Opening Your Class With Learning Stations

by Kim Marshall
with the editors of LEARNING magazine

LEARNING Handbooks
530 University Avenue
Palo Alto, California 94301

Foreword

Openness without chaos, independent learning with curriculum structure—these are the goals of a *Learning Stations* classroom. The practical suggestions in this handbook will help you develop a classroom where students' individual needs are met and teachers are free from the limitations of stand-up teaching.

The purpose of this and other LEARNING Handbooks is to help make teaching and learning more effective, interesting and exciting. Kim Marshall is a middle school teacher and has published a variety of magazine articles and books. His extensive experience has been combined with LEARNING magazine's research facilities and editorial depth to produce this down-to-earth and lively handbook.

EDITOR: Carol B. Whiteley
DESIGNER: David Hale
ILLUSTRATIONS: Frances Angelesco
PHOTOGRAPHY: Kim Marshall
COVER PHOTOGRAPH: Ken Sherman

EXECUTIVE EDITOR: Morton Malkofsky
DESIGN DIRECTOR: Robert G. Bryant

Library of Congress Number: 75-12462
International Standard Book Number: 0-915092-07-7

Book Code: 009 • Second Printing May 1976

Contents

On the Way to an Open Classroom

The open classroom burst onto the American scene of the 1960s as
the savior of public education. And while this teaching approach
has been victimized by overly romantic thinking and sloppy execu-
tion and has been turned upon by some parents and administrators
who view it as a noisy, undirected alternative to teaching kids the
important basic skills, many teachers recognize the soundness of
open education ideals and want to move in their direction. The problem is that without a very special teacher and without a group of
very special students, the open classroom fulfills the worst prophe-
cies of its critics.

The open classroom needs students who can work without the
constant supervision and help of the teacher, who can relate peacefully to each other without iron discipline. Open classrooms also
need individualized learning materials that have clear and simple
directions, interesting content and free the teacher to meet individual needs. Most textbooks meet none of these requirements, and
adequate non-textbook materials are only just beginning to appear
on the market. Open classroom teachers thus face the job of tracking
down those that are good and writing their own materials to fill in
the gaps. This requires energy, writing talent and plenty of time.

A further problem is that many schools don't fund the open classroom adequately, since they aren't geared to purchasing non-textbook materials. Again, teachers must either improvise their own materials or buy them out of their own pockets—another extra demand on talent and/or personal finances.

Yet another requirement of a good open classroom is that it have the support of parents and administrators. But open classroom teachers have to defend their different ways, and only those with exceptional charm and articulateness stand a chance of selling their methods to skeptical audiences.

Finally, running a successful open classroom requires different teaching skills, techniques and attitudes than those appropriate for stand-up teaching. Special training is usually needed, but with few good training or in-service programs in open education, the burden is once again on the teacher to be something special.

LEARNING STATIONS—THE MIDDLE ROAD

Given these conditions, it's not surprising that many dedicated teachers have burned themselves out after two or three years of exhausting creative effort in their open classrooms. Many have turned away from open education with a feeling of disillusionment and inadequacy, or hesitated at even beginning to open up their classrooms. It's clear that there is need for a middle ground, for methods that open the structured classroom from fear and authoritarianism and structure the open classroom so it's more orderly and rigorous. Many of us want to satisfy this need and help create conditions in which the best ideals of open education will flourish. But we need specific methods and programs to enable us to do a first-rate job.

Teachers all over the country have been working on such methods, trying to resist the swing back towards traditional education. For the past five years I have been working with a system called learning stations. It provides order and structure, yet leaves the teacher free to be creative and resourceful; it is a way station to a more open, individualized classroom. Learning stations is a system that *compresses* basic skills work into a shorter period of time (leaving more time open for other activities), *urges* kids who are behind to catch up with their peers (while providing plenty of help and a supportive climate), *liberates* most kids (especially those who are more self-motivated) to get involved in projects and activities in their free time and *motivates* just about everyone. It gets kids working at their full capacity, learning just as much as they can. What follows is an explanation of that system. I hope you will see in it elements that you can adopt or adapt to meet your own special classroom needs.

The What and Why of the Station System

I launched learning stations at the beginning of my second year of teaching. The idea was that kids would circulate around the class-room to different learning centers (I took the subjects I taught—math, English, social studies, spelling, reading—and carved them into five "stations," plus a general and a review station [science and art were handled by visiting specialists]), doing an assignment or a project at each one and moving on until they had completed all of them. When the assignments had been finished, the kids would have free time. The system was an instant success—the kids liked the freedom and the indirect responsibility for finishing the work by the end of the day. I felt liberated from the tight routine of stand-up teaching, and able to take part in individual teaching encounters around the room.

After a few weeks, however, I found that the system had two basic weaknesses: first, there were real traffic problems with twenty-five kids constantly moving from one center to another, and second, kids wanted to sit in one place with their friends. So, I adapted: I put the assignments (worksheets, pages in a book and activity cards for hands-on projects and experiments) in pockets around the room, and had the kids collect them all at once in a kind of elaborate ballet and then settle into groups to do their work. Friends could sit together, but the same basic rules applied: they could do the assignments in any order they liked, as quickly or as slowly as they wished, with as many or as few rest stops and as much or as little help as they needed—as long as they finished and handed in all seven by the end of the day.

Over the years my learning station system evolved into a general strategy for opening up and managing a self-contained classroom. As it operates in my classroom now, the system has five components:

1. feedback on the previous day's work (group or individual)
2. a class meeting
3. the learning station time
4. free time
5. a quiet reading time

This routine is used Monday through Thursday. It changes slightly on Friday when kids are group-tested in a conventional format on the main skills and concepts covered during the week.

The core of the system is the two- or three-hour block of learning station time—the other components support this time with feedback, a meeting to pull kids together as a group, free time to act as a cushion and an incentive and a time for quiet reading. For most of the day, the class is effectively decentralized. The teacher's role is not to teach one subject or control kids from the front of the room—instead it is to move around and deal with kids at an individual level. Kids aren't supposed to sit quietly and pay attention to a stand-up performance; they're expected to get involved in the work, plan their time so they will finish all of it and ask for help when they don't understand something. The system is more structured than the open classroom by virtue of the fact that kids do the same work and are required to finish it all by the end of the day. While worksheets during the week aren't for credit, they prepare the student and lead to conventional tests on Friday.

FREE TIME AND INDIVIDUALITY IN EXCHANGE FOR HARD WORK

Teaching in a learning station class is not easy—it requires energy and sensitivity. But the system demands less than charismatic presence or superhuman energy because it all but does away with stand-up teaching, and limits the work to one set of finite assignments. By compromising between conventional and open methods, learning stations avoids most of the discipline hassles and chaos inherent in those methods and does a great deal to decentralize and humanize a classroom. There's something appealing to most kids about being given the whole day's work at once and being able to manage their own time; they're out from under the constant supervision of the teacher, yet have a concrete challenge; they're able to talk and work with their friends, ask the teacher questions privately and enjoy some free time after finishing all their work. It strikes most kids as being a fair deal: hard work and responsibility in exchange for a more casual atmosphere and some free time. The system is simple, but the effects on the dynamics of a classroom are truly dramatic.

There's an important psychological advantage to a system like learning stations which may effect the way many kids work. When kids are allowed to do their work in their own private sequence and at their own speed, they escape the lock step of the whole class doing something together—a pattern against which spirited and independent kids are almost obligated to rebel. With six or seven learning assignments being done simultaneously, kids feel much more as though they are on their own. They still know, however, that everyone must complete the same body of work by the end of the day, and this produces a hidden group spirit. It's like the difference between marching a group of kids through a meadow in single file and telling them they can choose their own route as long as they all meet on the other side. Kids' experiences may not be that different and they are still going to the same place, but the restrictions chafe less and there's much more opportunity for human contact and individual ways of exploration and navigation.

Most kids respond quickly to the system by putting in really concentrated work in return for the free time and the satisfaction of getting the work done on their own. It's not uncommon for kids in a station class to work straight through recess and be reluctant to go to lunch—the system is a challenge and a powerful motivation. It's also common to see kids eager to get help and ask questions—they want to get the answers and understand the assignments because the incentives of the system have gotten them involved in the process of learning.

GROUP WORK LEADS TO COOPERATION AND FRIENDSHIP

When you let kids work in groups with their friends, you have opened your classroom to one of the most effective teaching devices—kids helping and prodding and pacing each other. It doesn't take kids long to form groups and read to each other, compare results and get into a group spirit about the work—it's often enough to make even division of decimals fun. Working in groups can help "problem" children learn to love school, redirecting their energy after years of negative, disruptive classroom antics.

Many of us talk about the value of kids building close friendships and learning how to live together, and it seems as though elementary classrooms are the ideal environment for kids to go through this crucial process—classrooms are more sheltered and controlled than the streets, but usually more open and diverse than the home. Many conventional classrooms, however, just don't have the time to let this all happen. Aside from the many academic benefits, a learning stations classroom enables human relations to grow. Kids get daily practice in getting along with each other in an open but carefully monitored environment, and the work lends itself to cooperation and participation. The result, if you handle the situation well, is that friendships form thick and fast, becoming much closer than those in the no-talking, listen-to-the-teacher environment of most conventional classrooms. Shy kids come out of their shells within the small, sheltered friendship groups; "troublemakers" lose their class-wide audience and find that the teacher-baiting game is harder to play and a waste of their working time—they, too, are likely to enjoy expressing themselves and showing off to a smaller group of friends while they all do their work. Outside the groups there is constant practice at settling disputes and learning how to avoid problems;

kids are always in contact picking up papers, moving around the room, sharpening their pencils, getting supplies and sharing resources in the free time. While there may be some confusion and conflict at first, kids are bound to work out their own ways of solving problems and getting along if you give them time and intervene strategically.

BUT HOW CAN I DO IT?

So far, the learning station system sounds good, but it raises a myriad of questions: How can you discipline kids without being directly in charge of what they are doing? Can you trust kids while allowing them freedom? How can you keep the noise from getting out of hand? Won't kids just copy off each other's papers? What happens if they rush through their work so they can have more free time? What happens when kids refuse to do their work, or do nothing but disrupt the class in their free time? How can you justify letting kids have any free time when there is so much to learn? How can you cover the required curriculum with such a short work time? How can you get through correcting seven assignments per child per day? Can individual needs really be met by just one set of assignments for everyone? Where are the self-instructing materials going to come from?

The rest of this book will attempt to answer these and other questions, or at least suggest ways you can answer them yourself. The learning station system is only one approach—which parts of it you can use will depend on many things: your own teaching style and the kind of school you work in, the ecology of your classroom, the ability of your kids to work independently, the availability of good individualized materials, adequate funding, the support of parents and administrators and your own training. But reading about the learning station system should help you to shape your own, individual system.

Discipline and the Learning Environment

The proper working environment in a classroom is a very subjective thing—one person's busy hum is another person's chaos; one person's freedom is another's anarchy. To adjust the level of activity so it's acceptable to your students and to you, it's necessary to know what components of the station system are influencing basic order.

The very act of decentralizing a classroom and allowing kids to work in groups defines many traditional discipline problems out of existence: the focus moves from the front of the room into each small group around the room; the teacher doesn't need iron control over every move and whisper and gives the responsibility for getting the work done and asking the right questions to the kids. It no longer should be against the rules to get up and sharpen a pencil, talk to a friend, or take a break from the work without permission—none of this stops the work from getting done or is a threat to your authority or effectiveness. Because you are circulating, dealing with kids individually, there is every chance that attention-getting kids will get attention without having to act up in front of the whole class; you are also likely to be able to anticipate many crises and hassles before they become disruptive.

Decentralizing the class also avoids discipline problems by helping

15

to create a warm, relaxed, friendly environment, one which is not conducive to conflict and tension. Because you don't have to keep everyone's attention on you at the front of the room, you don't have to be the bad guy all the time—there's no constant need to tell kids to sit down, stop talking and pay attention. Once you and the kids are used to stations and working in groups, the room mellows and develops a pace of its own. It becomes possible for you to talk to your students as individuals and allow a more friendly and relaxed side of yourself to emerge. That side will probably be more effective in getting kids to work harmoniously than any form of harsh authoritarianism.

ADJUSTING THE REQUIREMENTS

There are five key elements in the learning station system that you can tinker with to adjust the level of activity and accomplishment in the room:

1. the requirement that kids finish all the work
2. the difficulty of the work
3. the amount of work that has to be finished
4. the composition of the friendship groups
5. the tone and methods you use to handle conflict

In a class where kids are not used to working on their own and don't have a self-sustaining interest in doing school work, the requirement that they finish all stations may be the most important thing holding the class together. It is the crux of the kids' new responsibility for managing their own day's work. Ideally, this element of compulsion should be supplanted by a genuine interest in the work and a desire to do it for its own sake. But kids who have always been required to do school work may need months, even years of unlearning before they become self-motivated. In a station classroom, there is incentive to sit down and get the work done, not fool around and give the teacher a hard time. The work itself acts as a stabilizing and controlling force, and getting the work done becomes part of what motivates kids, rather than something to be delayed or avoided.

If the work in the learning stations is too hard for too many kids in the room, the stability and calm can begin to come unstuck—there will be too much demand for your attention, too much frustration, too many kids not doing their work as they wait for help. If the work is too easy, however, kids may not feel enough of a challenge and may have too much free time to handle constructively. Adjusting the difficulty of the work is an important part of keeping the classroom running smoothly. That is why it's good to plan the curriculum on a day-by-day basis to start with, getting a feel for the level the kids find challenging but not too frustrating. It's also something to keep in mind as you look for and write materials—besides covering the subject matter, your assignments should be clear and understandable, so most of your kids can work independently while you help those who need it. (See Chapter 5 for more on writing worksheets.) The level of work you can put in the learning stations should steadily rise during the year as your kids improve their skills, grow in independence and learn how to get help from their friends.

The difficulty of the work must also be influenced by the kids who find reading a painful and frustrating process. These kids are often those with the greatest potential for disrupting the system or forcing you into a negative discipline stance unless they are fully involved in the learning process. Therefore, the more students like this you have, the more important it is that there are some assignments and activities that slow readers can do without too much difficulty and that the rest of the work is within their reach if explained carefully on an individual basis. If much of the class can do the work on their own, you'll have much more time to spend with slow readers.

If there's too much work to finish by the end of the day, kids won't have any free time and will get bogged down and frustrated. But if there is too little work, kids may not be sufficiently challenged and may have too much free time on their hands (and you may have trouble justifying your system to parents and administrators). Again, you should adjust the amount of work to your own class at any given point in the year, and plan on a day-by-day basis until you get the right balance of work and free time. I have found that seven typewritten worksheets are about right for most of my own classes, but your situation may be quite different. Make sure there's time to get around to the kids who work more slowly and to help them arrange to sit with faster-working friends who will help them.

KEEP THE FRIENDSHIP GROUPS VIABLE

The friendships that kids form within the learning station classroom are a stabilizing factor. The more kids work and talk with the friends in their group, the less susceptible they are to distractions and disruptions around the room—and the happier and more productive they will be. But groups of friends can also be a problem if they become too boisterous and excited or if there are jealousies and conflicts within them. If this problem occurs, judicious, firm intervention on your part (splitting up groups, suggesting new groups, encouraging groups to include lonely kids) can prevent further trouble or hurt feelings. At the beginning of the third or fourth week of the year, and whenever things begin to come unstuck, ask the kids to write down the four other people in the room they would most like to sit with and give the piece of paper to you without showing it to anyone else. Take the papers home and try to arrange groups that match personalities in a harmonious way. Even if problems don't arise, you might want to go through this process many times during the year as kids change, friends split up and new students come into the room.

KEEPING YOUR COOL—THE CLASS MEETING AND THE CONFERENCE

No matter how well you adjust these four elements, there are still likely to be moments when you get angry at individual kids or feel like shouting at the whole class. It's at moments like these that the kids will watch you very carefully and learn from the way you handle yourself. A lot of what you're working to accomplish in this kind of classroom may be defeated if you are loud and impatient and authoritarian in moments of tension. Of course there are situations when time pressure, real chaos or the threat of immediate danger demand loud and emphatic intervention by the teacher, and nobody is saying that you shouldn't make your personal feelings known to your students. But it seems that the best way to solve problems and crises is with calm and rational discussions, whenever it's possible.[1]

There are two forums for applying non-authoritarian methods: the daily class meeting and the individual conference. The class meeting is the place to discuss any problem or project and arrive at a negotiated solution that satisfies as many as possible. Its ultimate objective is for kids to learn to solve their own problems instead of having solutions imposed on them. (See Chapter 7 for more on class meetings.)

While class meetings take place at a time separate from the learning station time, the work period and free time period provide ideal climates in which you can deal with problems on an individual or small group basis. When there is a fight, a loud argument, a refusal to do work or some other disruptive or defiant act that can't be ignored or solved by the kids themselves, you can take the kids involved aside and talk quietly and privately with them. The rest of the class should be able to continue their work without your direct supervision; if they're sufficiently absorbed in their work, many kids may not even notice that anything is happening. Since your conference is private, it's easier for both you and the kids involved to back down

---

[1]Dr. Thomas Gordon's *Teacher Effectiveness Training* (New York: Wyden, 1974) has some excellent ideas and methods in this area.

and save face if need be. And the fact that it's harder for disruptive kids to get the attention of the class makes them less likely to act out their problems so vocally. While the rest of the class continues with its work, you have the ideal setting for an effective conference—no audience, a one-to-one meeting and an implicit deadline, since the kids know there's work to be done.

SETTING A GOOD EXAMPLE

How calm and patient and issue-oriented you are in solving crises is vital to the stability of the classroom—over a period of months, quiet and effective methods should lead kids to imitate them in their own relationships and enable them to solve more and more of their own problems. In a station class, you lower your profile from that of a stand-up teacher, but you are still responsible for keeping things going well. Your role is basically passive yet you should be available to help or intervene anywhere and anytime it's necessary.

Sometimes it may be hard for you to relinquish the spotlight (teachers need attention too!). I often find myself giving too many lectures to the whole class, fussing loudly over little things, calling to kids across the room when I should go over and talk to them quietly and generally raising my voice too much. The example the teacher sets effects the whole class. If the teacher shouts, the kids are more likely to shout; if the teacher's temper is on a short fuse, the kids are more likely to blow up at each other over little things; if the teacher is hyperactive and impatient, the kids are likely to follow suit; if the teacher expresses anger in a blaming way and doesn't clearly state what caused it, the kids are more likely to react negatively and not get involved in solving the problem. But if we're consistently patient and calm and express our anger in a direct, matter-of-fact way, our kids are bound to be influenced, making the tone of our classrooms more civilized and peaceful.

Even when the work is at the right level of difficulty and the right amount, 10 or 15 kids may suddenly encounter a problem and all need help at once. If they can't get through to you, they may start grumbling about that teacher who "never helps me." If this happens, explain your position and ask the kids to go on to an easier paper (or get help from a friend) until you can get to them. Talk with one child at a time, in the order they asked for help; try to talk with the kids at their seats, rather than having them crowd around you. If this doesn't solve the problem, maybe the work is too hard, in which case a quick bit of stand-up, razzle-dazzle teaching may be needed to set everybody straight. You may also want to find better materials or rewrite them yourself.

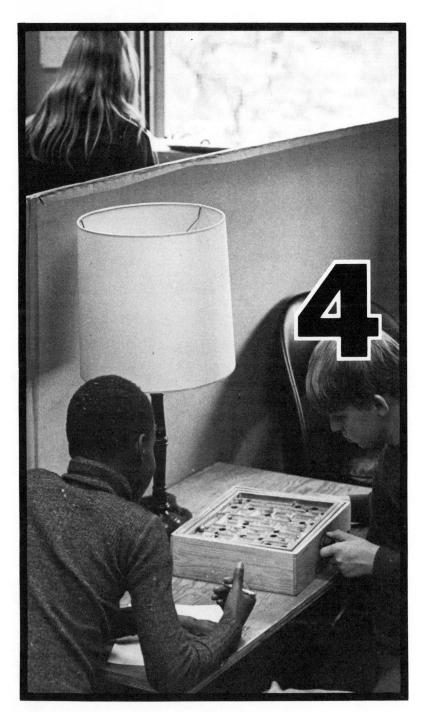

Noise and the Physical Setting

It's easy for kids who have come from strict, traditional classrooms to become noisy and overly excited in a more open setting. Unless there are some controls, a learning station classroom can present you with a major noise problem: kids talking loudly to people right next to them, shouting across the room, running around, clamoring for help. With 25 or 30 kids carrying on in an acoustically live room, noise can build on itself; as it becomes louder, kids have to talk more loudly to be heard, the teacher begins shouting and the sound level can change from a busy hum to an uncomfortable, negative din that distresses everyone.

It might seem logical to anticipate this problem by enforcing a strict rule of silence or "whispering only" during the station time. But if the room is really quiet, kids may feel self-conscious about asking questions or reading out loud to you or to each other. Too much attention may be focused on small interruptions, such as kids sharpening pencils, knocks on the door or people moving around the room. The atmosphere may become brittle and unsettled and keep kids from getting involved in their work and their group. In short, many of the most important benefits of a station system may be lost if you enforce a strict rule of silence.

It seems to me that a busy hum of noise, rather than silence, makes a better working environment. The low level of noise masks the inevitable interruptions and allows kids to talk to you and to each other without becoming the focus of class attention. A moderate buzz of noise smoothes the rough edges and stops you and the kids from battling over keeping the room silent. It also helps kids overcome their shyness or modulate their desire for attention.

Should you make yourself responsible for keeping the noise at a low buzz, intervening if it rises beyond a certain point? Again, it seems logical that you should be the enforcer—but there are three problems with this idea: (1) your teaching (consisting of countless individual conferences with kids all around the room) will be constantly interrupted as you have to shout and reprimand noisemakers; (2) you will get back into the "bad guy" role and some kids are bound to challenge and test you; (3) the kids won't have any responsibility for something that vitally affects them.

THE CLASS MEETING—A DECISION GROUND
There are a number of ways to deal with too much noise that are more effective than shouting, reprimanding and punishing. The most important thing in all solutions is that noise be a regular topic in class meetings from the very beginning of the year, and that a consensus is reached that too high a level of noise is bad for everyone (something kids will readily agree with, even the kids who are making most of the noise). Then, together, you can decide on a recognized, quiet way of signaling that the volume has to be turned down to a level that is acceptable to everyone (flipping the light switch, ringing a bell or quietly passing the word around. If necessary, the signal for quiet can be followed by a silent, five-minute cooling-off period or a class meeting to discuss the problem). If you and your class arrive at a level of noise that is acceptable to everyone but one or two kids, it's not ludicrous to consider earplugs as a solution.

Kids usually want to put the burden back on you, asking you to punish the noisy kids. But you have to point out that in opening up the room you have given them a lot of responsibility—that in exchange for the exceptional freedom they have in the room, they should learn to control themselves without your constant supervision. If you are called on to quiet down the whole class or a few recalcitrants, it should be because the kids want it quieter, not because you are saying that's the way it's going to be. Again, the best strategy is to go straight to the source of the problem—give attention to or help kids who directly or indirectly are showing a need for it, and calmly talk out the disputes that are raising voices. You can act as a model for everyone by projecting a soft-spoken, friendly and patient manner.

MUFFLE OR MASK

The poor acoustics of many classrooms can be dealt with in two ways: licking them or joining them. The first involves softening the hard surfaces of the room so that sounds don't bounce around as much. Architects tell me that the floor is the most important part of the room to soften (with thick carpeting) because it acts as a sounding board for noises. But walls, ceilings, blackboards and windows are also great reflectors and amplifiers of noise; it may be well worth it to ask your school to invest in acoustical tile for the ceiling, large sheets of cork or material for some of the vertical surfaces and curtains for the windows.

The "join 'em" approach to noise is to introduce other noise to the room which effectively mingles with and masks the noises you and the kids are making. Soft music, an air conditioning unit and electronic "white sound" are all effective in modulating noises and distractions. I've even heard of teachers recording the sound of hundreds of kids talking in their cafeteria and playing the tape back at low volume in a classroom—they said it worked beautifully!

Muffling or masking noise can help, but the two most important factors in noise abatement are still (1) kids taking some responsibility for monitoring themselves, and (2) the teacher setting an example by projecting an air of patience and calm. No matter what brings about quiet, it is important that you reinforce in kids' minds the moments when you think things are going really well—draw attention to harmonious times and compliment the class on how it is handling itself.

A WORKABLE ENVIRONMENT

Another part of getting a station system working smoothly is the way you arrange the room. Since there's bound to be a steady stream of people sharpening pencils, visiting, picking up work and getting books or games, it's important that kids can move easily around the room without bumping into other people or disturbing groups. The groups should be dispersed through the room so the noise is spread out. It's also vital to have a quiet corner with a rug and cushions (and chairs and a sofa if possible) which is physically cut off from the main part of the room by shelves or partitions, allowing kids to retreat from the hurly-burly of the classroom if they so desire. Study carrels and "forts" of various kinds can serve the same purpose. And if you have the time, energy and money, building a loft can add another dimension and lots more space to your room.

ROOM ARRANGEMENTS

The following diagrams show several possible arrangements for fourteen trapezoid tables in a room with a reading corner. Each arrangement is designed for a specific set of activities and tries to take advantage of the space in the room and the way the tables fit together. Of course, single-student desks can be moved into any of these arrangements too, and in some cases they are more flexible than trapezoid tables.

Kids need practice before they can transform the room from one configuration to another without a lot of noise and confusion. It's important to explain the purpose of the different arrangements (i.e., it's easier to see other people and share things in a circle, it's easier to see the speaker in a lecture format, etc.); you might make diagrams or overhead transparencies that show where each kid's table ends up in the new arrangement.

Here are seven basic formats—you'll probably think of several more.

1. **LEARNING STATION FORMAT**—In this arrangement, groups of four to six kids can work on individual assignments, group projects or book reading.

2. **LECTURE FORMAT**—This format is best for razzle-dazzle performances, visitors, overhead transparency viewing and other teacher-centered activities where kids need to have a writing surface in front of them. If they don't need to write, they can get closer to the action by pushing the desks aside and pulling their chairs into a tighter amphitheater arrangement.

3. **CLASS MEETING FORMAT**—A large circle seems to work best for meetings since there is no front and no back to the class and nearly everyone can see everyone else. The classic class meeting arrangement is just chairs pulled into a circle—but while this may be more intimate, some kids might be less shy sitting behind a circle of desks.

4. **TWO CIRCLES**—Trapezoid tables are at their best here because they fit together so neatly. This arrangement is good for play reading and other activities where the class is divided in two.

5. **TWO PROJECTS GROUPS**—This arrangement is best for art and social studies projects because it gives kids large amounts of table space.

6. **TESTING FORMAT**—Everyone is separated here and working alone. The tables needn't be lined up this way—most of the time I just let kids push out of their small learning station groups and the desks are higglety-pigglety all over the room.

7. **PARTY AND GAME FORMAT**—The decks are cleared for dancing, games, plays and other activities that need the maximum amount of open floor space.

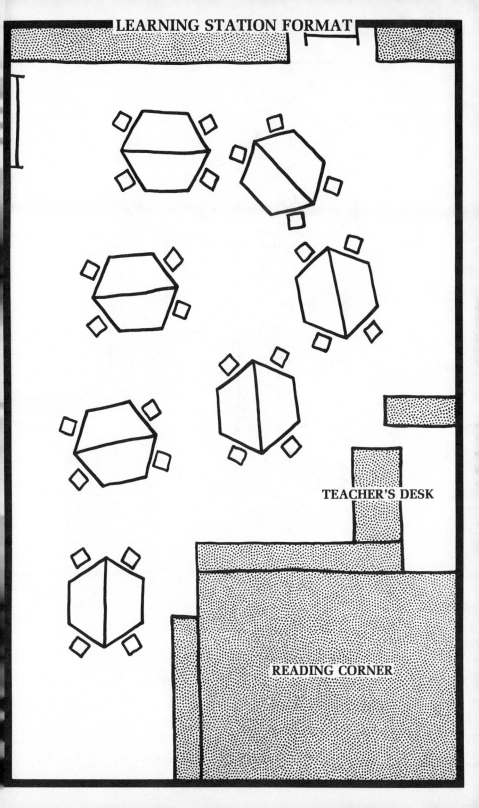

LEARNING STATION FORMAT

TEACHER'S DESK

READING CORNER

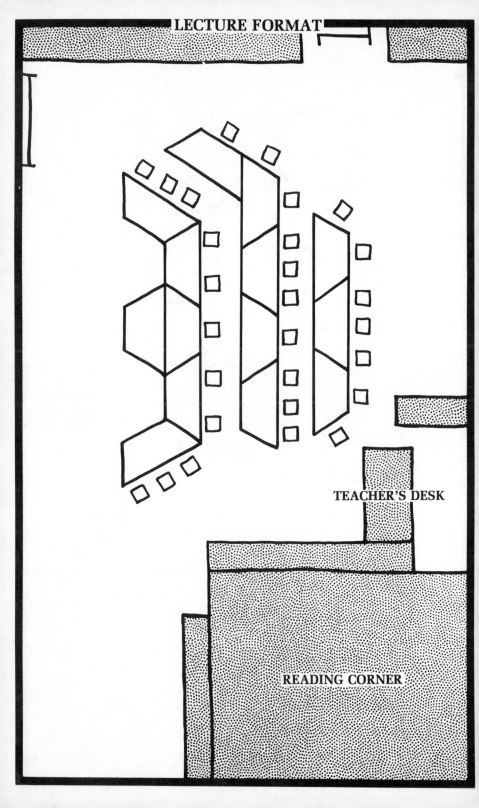

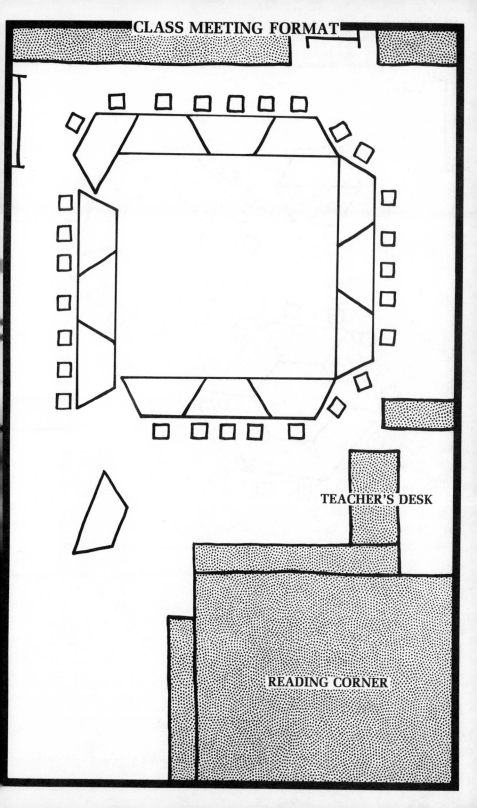

CLASS MEETING FORMAT

TEACHER'S DESK

READING CORNER

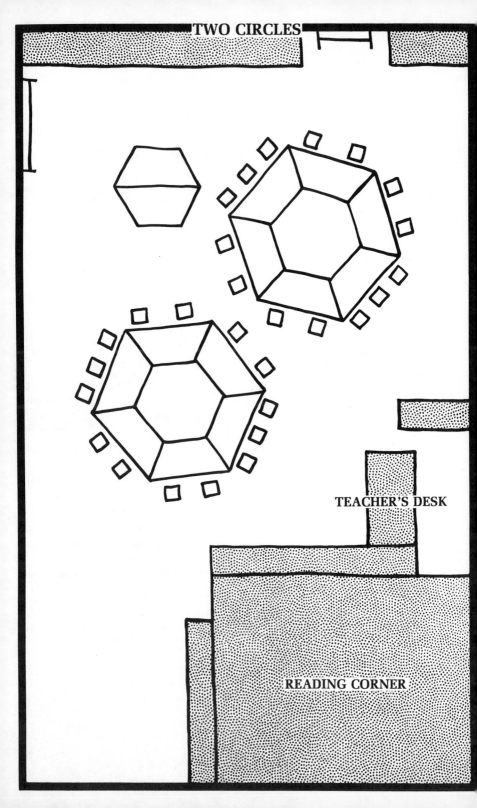

TWO CIRCLES

TEACHER'S DESK

READING CORNER

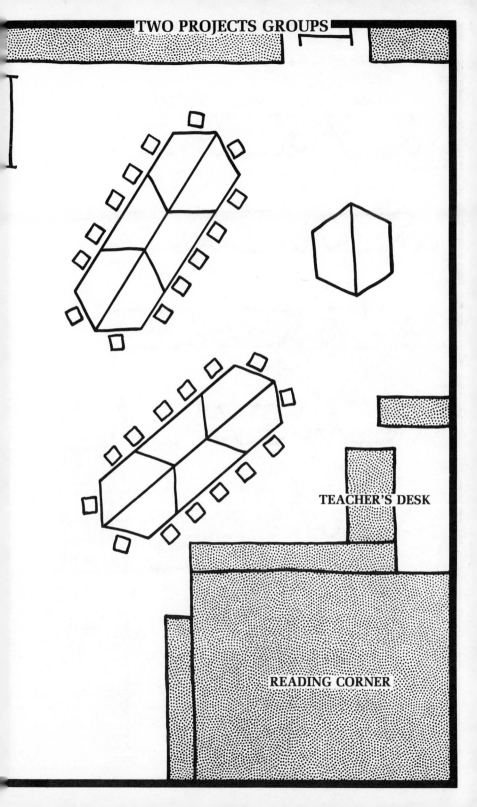

TEACHER'S DESK

READING CORNER

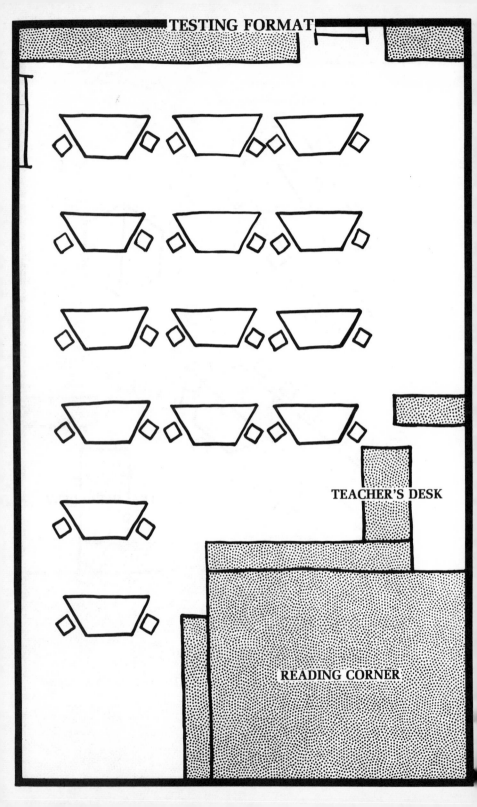

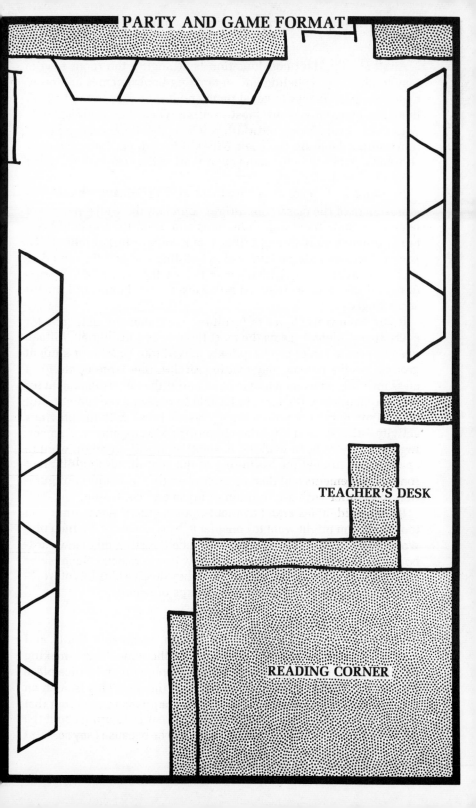

PARTY AND GAME FORMAT

TEACHER'S DESK

READING CORNER

Another important consideration is arranging the room so it is easy to clean up. Labeling and organizing books, games and other materials make it easy to get at them and just as easy to put back in the right place. Books are most inviting when they are displayed with their covers facing outward; you can label the books and put a number/title label on the shelf where they belong. Games always should be put back in the same open shelf so they can be checked at the end of each day.

Building and decorating ideas can also drastically change the atmosphere of the classroom. Bright colors on the walls, posters of famous personalities, wise quotations and beautiful art should certainly provoke more thoughts than blank walls or turkey cutouts. Of course the more kids are involved in building and painting and decorating and coming up with ideas and plans, the more likely they are to regard the room as theirs, a home away from home, and treat it accordingly.

If you have your choice of furniture, the trapezoid table (one for every two students) seems the most flexible and utilitarian. Fifteen or so trapezoid tables can be quickly moved into small four-student groups, twelve-person play-reading circles, one large circle for a class meeting, rows for a movie or an amphitheater arrangement for stand-up teaching. It's ideal to be able to re-shape the room to suit the activity going on, producing a physical break with the previous activity—this is most important in pulling kids together for a meeting after they've been working in small groups. You might want to spend some time at the beginning of the year discussing different room arrangements and then practice changing from one configuration to another with a minimum of noise and confusion.

If trapezoid tables aren't available and standard desks limit you too much, you might want to consider 8' by 4' sheets of 3/4-inch plywood (sanded and polyurethane-varnished) resting on heavy cardboard tubes from paper factories (usually free as rejects). Such tables can't be moved around very easily, but they do give kids lots of working space and provide a focus for groups of friends.

IT TAKES COOPERATION

Maintaining peace, keeping noise within acceptable limits and arranging the room properly are all part of the same thing—making the classroom a sympathetic learning environment and a nice place for everyone to spend almost six hours of the day. This is such an important goal and so much part of what happens in the room that it's tempting to use stern, authoritarian measures to bring about the right setting—"This is the way it's going to be because I say so." But such an approach is likely to bring resistance and lack of cooperation from kids who agree completely with what you're trying to accomplish—it may undermine the basic spirit of the system. Although it's time-consuming and cumbersome on the short run, involving your kids in identifying the problems and formulating the solutions is vital and gives you much more hopeful long-term prospects. Creating and maintaining a good learning environment should be a cooperative venture, and should bring about a feeling of group pride. It can enable you to shift responsibility to the kids and begin the process of making them independent, motivated learners.

The Curriculum

I teach in an inner-city school in which the textbooks available turn kids off with overly difficult vocabulary and Dick-and-Jane interests; it is completely impossible for me to run a learning station classroom giving assignments from these textbooks. Since the unspoken message from administrators and supervisors in my school is that I can pretty much use whatever materials I want, as long as I teach basic skills, keep the peace and use materials that don't offend anyone, I have been writing my own curriculum, using every source at my disposal—textbooks, workbooks, curriculum guides, newspapers, magazines, movies, books and television. Since I try to keep away from all-class instruction and move around to meet individual needs, I expect all the materials and projects and manipulatives I use at the stations to meet five basic requirements:

1. They must have clear directions and proceed in carefully graduated steps; most kids should be able to learn from them with only occasional help from the teacher.

2. The materials and projects must be interesting and relevant enough to combat boredom and provide motivation; kids should be able to get involved in them and resist the temptation to slough off or copy their neighbor's work. The teacher can provide a lot of the

excitement and motivation needed in a classroom, but the materials must play a bigger part in a decentralized class where the teacher is doing less performing at the front of the room.

3. Materials have to teach basic skills and fulfill school requirements. If they don't, the teacher may be vulnerable to attack from skeptics who are suspicious of the openness and free time in the class. This means that research must be done to find the minimum requirements of the school and locate (or create) the materials that meet them.

4. Materials should cover the subject matter at a reasonable pace; the work at any given moment shouldn't be too demanding or intense for most kids to do on their own.

5. As many of the materials as possible should have self-checking mechanisms built into them; this enables kids to get a pretty good idea of how they are doing *as they work*, rather than having to wait to get back corrected papers later. (For more on effective feedback, see Chapter 6.)

ADAPTING TO MEET YOUR SITUATION

Depending on the degree of independence of your kids, the demands of parents and administrators and your school's policies on requiring textbooks or specific programs, the materials you use may not be able to meet these criteria. If you're required to use materials that aren't self-instructing for most students, you may want to make some changes in your use of the learning station system:

1. You might want to introduce new concepts with a day of stand-up teaching and then use a decentralized format for the remaining days of the week or unit.

2. You might want to explain out loud each learning station at the beginning of every day before opening up the class.

3. You might want to stagger the days on which new concepts are introduced so all units don't begin on the same day; this would give you more time to answer questions on the new unit while the other subjects were more or less self-instructing. This approach would mean staggering the tests as well, perhaps having a learning station time every day of the week and having one test at the beginning of each day, rather than having all tests on Friday.

4. You might want to use learning stations only one or two days a week and teach conventionally the rest of the time.

If you are required to use materials that you think aren't interesting, you may want to supplement them with your own worksheets or projects. You might have kids circulate through a learning center with manipulatives or pictures or a calculator or books;

everyone in the room would be able to get up close to them by the end of the day, and have a more direct learning experience.

Any of these adaptations might be further adaptable as your kids get the knack of working and figuring things out on their own; part of using the system effectively is being open to changes as the class develops during the year.

THE ONE-WEEK UNIT

A lot of the work involved in writing my own curriculum has been spent carefully breaking down the subject matter into manageable, bite-sized chunks. I have come to rely quite heavily on a one-week unit in math, English, social studies and spelling, with four days of worksheets (which I write myself) culminating in a test on the fifth day. My selection and organization of topics have centered around what my kids could learn in those four days. By way of example, the following are one-week units I have developed for my sixth grade classes:

MATH
1. writing numbers as words
2. place value to trillions
3. decimal place value to thousandths
4. one-number division
5. two-number multiplication
6. three-number multiplication
7. two-number division
8. three-number division
9. multiplication of decimals
10. division of decimals
11. graphing, using manipulatives
12. graphing, plotting coordinates
13. names of parts (addend, product, etc.)
14. factors and primes
15. prime factors; factor trees
16. rounding numbers off, decimals
17. ratios
18. exponents
19. finding the average
20. Roman numbers
21. measurement, time, money, etc.
22. fractions—basic concepts
23. fraction equivalencies (½=2/4)
24. adding and subtracting unlike denominators

30. pronouns
31. adjectives
32. adverbs
33. articles and prepositions
34. conjunctions and interjections
35. sentence patterns
36. all parts of speech together

SOCIAL STUDIES
 1. reading map of the classroom
 2. reading map of corridor of school
 3. reading map of entire school
 4. reading map of area around school
 5. reading map of neighborhood of school
 6. reading map of Boston
 7. reading map of Greater Boston
 8. reading map of Massachusetts
 9. reading map of New England
10. reading map of the United States
11. reading map of North America
12. reading map of Western Hemisphere
13. reading map of Eastern Hemisphere
14. reading map of the world
15. review of all maps together
16. through 27. history units
28. ancient and modern cities
29. pollution problems
30. ecology problems
31. basic laws
32. forms of killing
33. fair and unfair laws
34. legal versus moral duties
35. moral dilemmas
36. projects

SPELLING
This station consists of a list of 900 words broken into 36 units of 25 words each. Each unit contains groups of associated words, homonyms, synonyms and antonyms and phonetic oddities. Here is how each one-week unit is structured:

Monday The first 12 words are introduced with informal, straight-talking definitions; kids use the words in sentences (or weave the words into a single story) and answer two or three questions on phonics.

Tuesday The remaining 13 words are introduced with definitions; kids use them in sentences or a story, answer two or three phonics questions and break the first 12 words into syllables in the Review Station (for more on the use of the Review Station, see page 42).

Wednesday All 25 words are in a box at the top of the worksheet, and kids write them by the proper definition down the page.

Thursday All 25 words are in a box again, and kids fill them into blanks in sentences, using only context clues. Also, the Review Station has the last 13 words to break into syllables, and the General Station has a word-search puzzle in which kids have to find, circle and write the week's 25 spelling words.

Friday Kids take a conventional test or write down sentences and paragraphs I dictate that include all 25 words.

Having the curriculum units laid out in advance for the whole year (and arranged around the school calendar so that objectives that take a short time to teach fall on weeks shortened by vacations) has freed me from much of the Sunday night panic about what we're going to be doing next week. It also allows me readily to defend the curriculum to skeptics. With the year plotted out, I can use my energy for other projects and creative departures, and concentrate more on meeting individual needs. Having units planned in advance doesn't preclude changing the order or even dumping certain units, nor does it limit my freedom or spontaneity—in fact, I'm convinced that it has increased my freedom of action by giving me more security and less vulnerability to conservative criticism.

THE ONE-DAY UNIT

The Reading, General and Review Stations more readily lend themselves to a single-worksheet, one-day approach than to week-long progressions culminating in tests. Here are some materials and activities I use at these stations:

READING Current news stories, poems, fables, movie plots, TV shows, song lyrics, personal experiences, class problems, adventure stories and cartoons work well at this station. I type the story or words down one side of the page, then ask a series of factual and open-ended questions down the other side. These worksheets can be cut in half vertically and used as tests, with kids reading the story and then answering the questions without looking back.

GENERAL This station is a catchall for one-time teaching ideas. I have used puzzles, word games, crossword puzzles, jokes, grouping exercises, analogies, hink pinks, questionnaires about the class, creative writing ideas one day a week, line drawings, jumbled sentences and words, word-search puzzles on Thursdays in conjunction with the Spelling Station, mazes, questions on posters and pictures on the walls, discussion ideas, moral dilemmas, values clarification and treasure hunts for information in books around the room.

REVIEW   The Review Station worksheet focuses on the skills that kids may forget soon after they've "learned" them. I rotate subjects during the week, with a cumulative review of all math skills covered up to that point on Mondays and Wednesdays and a similar review of English skills (including breaking that week's spelling words into syllables) on Tuesdays and Thursdays. On Fridays I give a cumulative math review test along with the regular unit tests in math, English, social studies and spelling.

The feeling of mastery of many different skills that comes from Review Station worksheets can be very exciting for kids—they may never before have had a grasp of such a broad array of facts and concepts at one time, and the chances that they'll remember them are excellent after six months of continuous review. I encourage kids to analyze their review papers so they'll zero in on their remaining weak points.

SHOULD YOU WRITE YOUR OWN WORKSHEETS?

Writing your own curriculum is in no way a prerequisite for running a learning station class. But in my particular situation, writing my own worksheets and creating my own projects and manipulatives have worked, and kids have responded very favorably. Here are some of the advantages I've found in teacher-written worksheets:

1. They're cheaper than textbooks, even with all the paper used (see page 44 of this chapter), theoretically leaving more of the classroom budget allocation to spend on paperbacks, trips, gerbils, rugs and so forth.

2. I know my students better than any textbook writer, and can come up with more relevant ways of explaining things.

3. I can inject humor, use the names of kids in my class, refer to incidents in the room, school and community and use zany graphics and lettering, making the subject matter less threatening and more fun to read and work with.

4. I can use a variety of materials (poems, stories, song lyrics, crossword puzzles, magazine articles, etc.) that would be costly to purchase in class numbers in their original form.

5. I can include news stories that happened as recently as the

night before, injecting relevance and immediacy into the curriculum.

6. I am very familiar with material I have written myself; this makes me more effective in answering and understanding work-related questions and problems.

7. I have much more freedom of style, sequencing and pacing in my teaching, opening up new opportunities for creativity.

8. I can learn from my own mistakes and improve my materials for the next year.

STARTING OUT

It may take you awhile to get the knack of writing interesting work-sheets. I got off to a shaky start and made plenty of mistakes, both in terms of typographical errors and in terms of misjudging the level of my students and trying to explain too much too quickly. I always suffered for the worksheets that were too hard by having to make my way through a blizzard of questions the next morning (sometimes I just called the class together and asked everyone to do the offending paper together with me). Gradually I got better at explaining things to the kids on paper in a way that made most of the worksheets really self-instructing. I found that even on Mondays, when I was introducing a new concept in math and English and starting up new units in social studies and spelling, I only had to explain things individually to about half the kids, while the rest figured their work out for themselves or picked it up from their friends. Most of the kids I did talk to individually only needed around thirty seconds or a minute of being led and prodded through the first two or three problems to get them working on their own, while only two or three kids required more sustained help to get through the material. After four years, I saw little good in rewriting a lot of the worksheets, so I wrote up polished versions and started Thermofaxing them.

One problem with a lot of published materials is that they assume previous knowledge and vocabulary that kids may not have. When I introduce new concepts, I always try to begin from scratch, assuming absolutely nothing, and work quickly up to grade level in the first two or three days of the unit. Starting at a very simple, graphic level doesn't hurt the brighter students, and greatly increases the possibility of slower kids grasping concepts for the first time.

One problem with writing your own materials is the amount of time it takes (up to 90 minutes a night)—this on top of the rather substantial amount of correcting involved in learning stations (see Chapter 6). There are two ways of cutting down on writing time: (1) share the job of writing materials with one or more colleagues and pool your output between your classes; (2) tackle one subject area a year while using conventional materials in the other subjects; produce polished, Thermofaxable materials in each area before moving on to another subject the next year.

Another problem may be mistakes and typographical errors in your materials, for which you may get flak from parents and administrators. You can capitalize on this possibility: make a game or activity for the kids of finding the errors. This can help many of your students to become expert proofreaders, and should make you a much more careful writer.

Writing your own worksheets will demand a great deal of paper. When faced with the bill for 72 reams of paper in one year (that's what 30 copies of seven worksheets per day adds up to), some conservative administrators may suddenly develop a concern for the nation's forests, and tell you to put your assignments on the blackboard. The most important thing to point out to people who criticize heavy paper use is that you are not using textbooks and standard ruled paper and may therefore be *saving* the school system money. You should point out the advantages of your worksheets, the greater involvement of students and the fact that they own and can write on their materials, rather than having to turn them back unmarked to the school. You may also want to argue that your paper should be deducted from your annual budget for educational materials, since you are printing your curriculum on that paper. Assuming that you have between $200 and $300 allocated to your class for a year, you should have a fair amount of money left over after buying paper to spend on other materials. You can argue that to teach properly, you must be supplied properly.

IF THE ANSWER IS NO, YOU CAN ADAPT

If skeptics of heavy paper use are adamant, you may have to abandon the ideal of one worksheet per subject per child per day, and compromise:

1. Use both sides of a sheet of paper, cutting paper consumption in half.

2. Write some of the shorter assignments on the board.

3. Print up enlarged copies of some assignments and put them at a learning center; have students circulate through the center during the day, putting their answers on blank paper (each single sheet of paper can accommodate answers for more than one assignment).

4. Make a transparency of a worksheet and use an overhead projector to project it on a screen.

5. Use substance 16 duplicating paper or newsprint paper, both of which are thinner and cheaper than the standard substance

20 paper.

6. Scrounge wastepaper from printing stores, offices and political campaign headquarters and use the backs.

7. Use project cards, laminated worksheets, long-range assignments or manipulatives—anything that doesn't require daily worksheets.

8. Get students involved in the spirit of conserving and re-cycling paper.

9. Buy some paper yourself.

DEVELOPING YOUR OWN STYLE

Whatever form it takes, the "formal" curriculum in a learning station classroom is only the beginning of what can happen and what can be learned. I should stress again that writing your own curriculum is not a prerequisite, that worksheets are only one of many ways of involving kids in learning at stations. You should search the market for materials that are self-instructing, motivating, that cover the curriculum effectively and are properly packaged and paced for your kids. But whatever materials you use, you will find you have much more time and energy to spare for exciting projects and group sessions, small group meetings, individual projects, field trips and so forth. Besides that, you'll find that the whole process encourages better human relations and interaction between kids, every minute of the day. In this kind of classroom it's possible to have the best of both worlds—the rigor of traditional classrooms and the informal learning possibilities of open classrooms. And all the time kids are being prepared to learn in less and less structured environments, to use the world as their classroom and life as their curriculum.

WORKSHEETS

The next eleven pages contain a representative sampling of learning station worksheets—hopefully they'll give you some idea of the kind of materials I've been working with in my own class, and of some of their strengths and weaknesses.

The first seven worksheets represent the major study blocks of a typical day—one worksheet each for math, English, social studies, spelling, reading, general and review, taken from different points in the week. The math sheet is the beginning of a unit on rounding off numbers. It is full of helpful props, but by the end of the week, kids should be able to round off numbers without any help from number lines or sentences or diagrams.

The English worksheet is the first assignment in a unit on forming the plural. It starts from scratch but becomes less structured during the week until the test on the fifth day asks kids to form plurals with no help at all.

The social studies worksheet is the second of a one-week unit on legal versus moral duty. It's straightforward, fill-in-the-blank style, but has an open-ended invitation at the end for kids to be creative.

The spelling worksheet is the fourth day of a 25-word, one-week unit. (Kids have used each word in their own sentences on Monday and Tuesday and matched the 25 words with their definitions on Wednesday.) The general worksheet is a puzzle with the same 25 spelling words hidden in a jumble of letters.

The reading worksheet is a write-up of an incident I saw reported in a newspaper. This kind of worksheet can be made a good deal easier for slow readers by reading it with them, and a good deal harder for fast readers by having them fold it vertically in half, read the story and then answer the questions without looking back at the text.

The review worksheet is not in sequence with the other worksheets—it is included here to give you an idea of what a final, year-end cumulative test looks like. During the year, a new skill gets added each week and old skills are repeated; in this way, kids get a firm grasp of the entire year's curriculum and are helped to maintain that grasp.

The other four worksheets show work being covered at various stations during the year.

Date: _____ MATH STATION   Name: _____

Rounding numbers off, 1

┌─────┐
│ 31 │
└─────┘

* Use the number line to round these numbers off
  to the nearest ten:

```
      60                    70                    80
  59 | 61 62 63 64 65 66 67 68 69 | 71 72 73 74 75 76 77 78 79 | 81 82 83 84 85 86 87
```

64 - ____ (is it closer to 60 or 70?)   69 - ____

76 - ____ (is it closer to 70 or 80?)   84 - ____

71 - ____   65 - ____

83 - ____   61 - ____

66 - ____   79 - ____

59 - ____   82 - ____

75 - ____ (5 goes up to the higher ten)   62 - ____

---

  * Now round these off to the nearest ten   ⟵ Down   up ⟶
    without using a number line. Remember,   1 2 3 4 5 6 7 8 9

46 - ____ (between **40** and **50** , closer to which?)

33 - ____ (between ____ and ____ , closer to which?)

94 - ____

22 - ____   88 - ____

16 - ____   51 - ____

54 - ____   45 - ____

55 - ____   87 - ____

99 - ____   22 - ____

---

* Now round these off to the nearest 100: (look at the tens place to decide)
↓
1̲4̲2̲ - ____ (between **100** and **200** , closer to which?)

489 - ____ (between ____ and ____ , closer to which?)

827 - ____

421 - ____

Plurals of nouns, 1

* Follow the rule for making the plural (more than one)
  of each group of nouns. Try to remember the rules.

I. Most words add s

garden - *gardens*

hen - _____

skyscraper - _____

singer - _____

table - _____

typewriter - _____

house - _____

car - _____

**II. Words ending in y change
the y to i and add es**

city - *cities*

country - _____

party - _____

lady - _____

navy - _____

candy - _____

**III. But words ending in ey
just add s**

valley - *valleys*

jockey - _____

monkey - _____

**IV. Words ending in f
change the f to v and
add es**

leaf - *leaves*

shelf - _____

half - _____

calf - _____

**V. Words ending in fe
change the f to v and
add s**

knife - *Knives*

wife - _____

life - _____

**VI. Words ending in o,
ss, sh, ch, and x
add es**

tomato - *tomatoes*

pass - _____

wish - _____

church - _____

fox - _____

potato - _____

dish - _____

tax - _____

mass - _____

latch - _____

**VII. And some are just
crazy and you have to
remember them!**

man - *Men*

woman - _____

child - _____

tooth - _____

goose - _____

mouse - _____

foot - _____

deer - _____

sheep - _____

ox - _____

Date:_____   SOCIAL STUDIES STATION   Name:_____

* Remember from yesterday: <u>legal duty</u> – the law says you must do it

                                      <u>moral duty</u> – you should do it, but you don't have to

* Say what kind of duty is
  involved in each case and
  answer the other question.

1. A woman is walking along a dark street late one night.
  Suddenly she is jumped by a man. He beats her and starts
  to strangle her. You are sitting watching this from your
  window. You have a telephone and know the number to call
  to get the police.

  Should you call the police? _____   What kind of duty? _____

2. A lifeguard is paid to watch people swimming at a beach.
  One afternoon he sees someone who seems to be drowning,
  but the lifeguard is busy talking to his girlfriend, and
  besides, the water is cold!

  Should the lifeguard save the person? _____   What kind of duty? _____

3. A teacher is driving down the street outside his school
  one afternoon after school. He sees a big crowd of kids
  from the school watching a fight between two boys. The
  teacher knows the kids and knows someone might get hurt.

  Should the teacher stop the fight? _____   What kind of duty? _____

4. The same teacher is on lunch duty the next day in the
  school cafeteria. Two kids bump into each other in the
  lunch line and start calling each other names. Pretty soon
  they are fighting, and one of them grabs a knife.

  Should the teacher stop the fight?_____   What kind of duty? _____

5. The firemen are sitting around the fire station near a
  school when they hear the alarm for the school go off.
  They know that the school has lots of false fire alarms
  being pulled all the time, so they decide not to go.

  Should the firemen go? _____   What kind of duty? _____

  Why? _____

  _____

6. People are starving right now in other countries. Should
  we send money to help them get food? _____

  Is that a moral or a legal duty (if you think so)? _____

7. A man (who happens to be an excellent swimmer) is
  walking beside a river when he hears cries for help and
  sees someone drowning in the river.

  Should he try to save the person? _____   What kind of duty? _____

** If you have time, make up a few stories of your own on the
  back and ask your friends what they think people should do
  in them.

Date: _____   SPELLING STATION   [25]   Name: _____

* Put each word in the right sentence.

right write alert closet debt scarce scared visitor unexpected arrest
murder bicycle liquor hockey clumsy orphan protect recover equator tough
jigsaw puzzle difficult vulture corpse donkey

1. He reminded me that I had a _____ of ten dollars to pay him.

2. In the city, a _____ can often go faster than a car.

3. That boy is so _____ that he tripped over his own feet.

4. The news of her father's death was completely _____ , and it shocked her badly.

5. The undercover policeman was able to _____ the drug pushers.

6. The weather near the _____ is very hot.

7. He wondered whether he had done the _____ thing reporting his friend.

8. _____ is a fast, exciting, and violent sport.

9. The _____ circled over the man waiting for him to die.

10. Food was very _____ during the long famine.

11. A person who can't _____ or read is called an illiterate.

12. The job of the Secret Service is to _____ the President of the U.S.A.

13. In most states you have to be 18 before you can buy _____ .

14. The woman hid in the _____ while the burglar searched the house.

15. The _____ with 500 pieces was driving them crazy.

16. Her mother's death made her an _____ at the age of ten.

17. The cowboys left the _____ of the horse to decompose in the desert.

18. The classroom had a _____ who stayed for the whole morning.

19. They used their _____ to carry food from the town.

20. She asked how long it would take her to _____ from the disease.

21. The girl was so _____ that nothing would make her cry.

22. "I can't do this work," he said. "It's too _____ ."

23. A soldier on guard duty had better be _____ all the time.

24. They were _____ to walk anywhere near the cemetery at night.

25. He was found guilty of _____ and given life in prison.

Date: _____   <u>READING STATION</u> | 12 | Name:_____

An Unidentified Flying Object?

In October of 1973, two men were sitting on a pier by the Mississippi River fishing. It was after dark, and they were just relaxing and having a good time. Suddenly the two men heard a strange buzzing noise across the water. They looked up and saw a strange blue object moving towards them. It didn't look like anything they had ever seen before — it looked like a spaceship.

The blue thing stopped a few yards away from them and hovered in the air, making the strange buzzing sound. Then a door opened in the side and three strange creatures came out. The men said these creatures didn't look like humans at all. The creatures didn't say anything, but one of them made a buzzing noise.

Before the men could run away, the three creatures grabbed them by their arms and carried them into the spaceship. But the creatures didn't hurt the men. They just looked at them very carefully. The two men said they got the feeling that they were being examined by some instrument, maybe a camera. After a few minutes the creatures let the men go, and the strange blue object flew away.

The men were left alone on the dark bank of the river. They were terrified. They knew they couldn't be dreaming because it had happened to both of them. The first thing they did was to take a good drink out of a whiskey bottle they had with them. Then they tried to figure out what they should do.

They knew that if they went and told people, no one would believe the story and everyone would laugh at them and say they were drunk or crazy. But the two men were sure that it had happened. They knew they weren't drunk or crazy.

Finally they decided it was their duty to tell the police what had happened — what if people from another planet were about to invade the Earth? So they went to the police station. The police questioned the men for a few hours and decided they were telling the truth. They even called in a doctor to see if the men were all right. The doctor said he thought the men were telling the truth.

Lots of newspaper reporters and people from radio and television interviewed the men, and all of them thought they were telling the truth. But there has been no sign of the spaceship since then, and nobody really knows.

Questions:

1. Why were the two men out by the river? _____

_____

2. What did they think the blue object was?_____

_____

3. Did the blue object touch the ground?_____

4. What word tells you?_____

5. What did the three creatures do to the men inside the spaceship?_____

_____

6. What was the first thing the two men did after this experience?

_____

7. Why? _____

8. Why were they afraid to tell people at first?

_____

_____

9. Why did they think it was their duty to tell the police?

_____

_____

10. Did the police and reporters believe the men?

_____

11. Do you believe their story?

_____

12. How do we know that they didn't just make up the whole story?

_____

_____

_____

_____

* Find this week's 25 spelling words, circle them, and write them on the right.

```
B  J  T  Z  B  L  J  K  Z  T  S  B  Z  T  L
C  V  M  C  Q  R  C  B  D  C  L  J  Q  R  A
B  I  T  R  C  Y  T  L  Q  N  A  H  P  R  O
R  S  B  D  E  C  M  D  U  Q  R  B  R  C  Q
R  I  C  K  E  C  M  B  D  M  L  E  U  Q  R
C  T  C  T  M  B  O  D  O  R  S  B  D  Q  R
C  O  O  B  C  M  J  V  Q  T  A  Y  B  C  D
H  R  E  J  Q  U  R  B  E  S  P  R  O  C  C
P  G  H  I  J  K  L  M  N  R  O  W  P  Q  S
E  R  D  S  T  U  T  H  G  I  R  V  W  C  C
Q  X  I  O  Y  A  Z  B  Z  I  T  J  A  L  A
U  P  F  B  N  J  L  R  T  H  O  R  O  D  R
A  A  F  L  O  K  V  E  E  S  E  S  K  I  C
T  M  I  B  C  Q  E  R  R  D  E  Q  B  D  E
O  O  C  J  B  X  M  Y  X  T  C  Z  P  Y  Z
R  B  U  J  C  D  Q  R  R  B  B  C  M  L  B
M  B  L  G  D  M  E  D  L  E  Z  P  R  I  B
Z  Q  T  R  H  D  C  T  Q  D  R  A  C  Q  B
C  M  B  X  R  B  D  M  C  X  J  Y  P  U  O
U  J  P  U  Z  S  T  P  L  E  C  M  B  O  T
S  J  M  Q  J  E  S  T  B  L  P  J  D  R  B
L  J  V  U  L  T  U  R  E  B  T  X  J  P  D
L  M  B  J  D  M  B  V  C  Q  R  B  E  D  L
M  B  D  M  C  Q  R  B  A  C  Q  R  E  N  O
U  B  E  L  Z  Z  U  P  W  A  S  G  I  J  U
```

1. _____
2. _____
3. _____
4. _____
5. _____
6. _____
7. _____
8. _____
9. _____
10. _____
11. _____
12. _____
13. _____
14. _____
15. _____
16. _____
17. _____
18. _____
19. _____
20. _____
21. _____
22. _____
23. _____
24. _____
25. _____

Date: end of year   REVIEW STATION   Name: _____

① Words: 701,000

_____

② Numbers: eight hundred billion

_____

③ Words: 9.3

_____

④ Numbers: twelve and eleven thousandths

_____

⑤ 9.35 + 81.664 = _____
⑥ 12.6 - 9.481 = _____
⑦ 835 × 7 = _____
⑧ 90.4 × .37 = _____
⑨ 6621 × 452 = _____
⑩ 3432 ÷ 6 = _____
⑪ 28.934 ÷ 3.4 = _____
⑫ 372354 ÷ 542 = _____
⑬ Factors of 40 _____ _____ _____
⑭ Round to the nearest thousand:
    12,563 - _____
⑮ Round to the nearest hundredth:
    .7348926 - _____
⑯ Ratio: 6:42 = 9:____
⑰ Nine cubed + four to the fourth =
    _____
⑱ Find the average of
    8, 6, 4, 2, and 5 - _____
⑲ MCMLXXIV - _____
⑳ Write Roman numerals for:
    3,269 - _____

㉑ What fraction? ⊘ —

㉒ $\frac{5}{6}$
    $-\frac{1}{4}$

㉓ To mixed:
    $\frac{12}{5}$ =

㉔ To improper: $9\frac{1}{2}$ =

㉕ $6\frac{4}{5}$
    $+7\frac{3}{5}$

㉖ $4\frac{1}{3}$
    $-1\frac{2}{3}$

㉗ Reduce: $\frac{12}{16}$ =

㉘ $\frac{6}{7} \times \frac{1}{3}$ =

㉙ $\frac{4}{7} \div \frac{1}{14}$ =

㉚ 3 is what percent of 15 _____
㉛ 75% of 60 = _____
㉜ How many dimensions? □ _____
㉝ What is the perimeter of a
    field 20 yards × 15 yards: _____
㉞ Area of the same field = _____
㉟ Volume of a box 12 inches long,
    3 inches wide, 5 inches high: _____
㊱ Circumference of circle radius 5" _____
㊲ Area of same circle: _____

Date: _____   MATH STATION   Name: _____

Rounding numbers off, 4 | 36 |

* Round to the nearest ten:	* Round to the nearest hundred:	* Round to the nearest thousand:	* Round to the nearest tenth:
24 - _____	746 - _____	8,324 - _____	↓ .24316 - ____
58 - _____	687 - _____	6,549 - _____	.67453 - ____
83 - _____	399 - _____	2,314 - _____	.54627 - ____
75 - _____	251 - _____	6,502 - _____	.24315 - ____
27 - _____	931 - _____	5,999 - _____	.79576 - ____
97 - _____	365 - _____	3,671 - _____	.24325 - ____
72 - _____	374 - _____	4,218 - _____	.87956 - ____

* Round to the nearest million:	* Round to the nearest billion:
4,354,678 - _____	↓ 8,342,576,887 - _____
3,654,890 - _____	1,546,887,593 - _____
2,246,111 - _____	3,555,476,998 - _____
8,795,253 - _____	7,324,154,734 - _____
14,365,666 - _____	9,763,656,259 - _____
57,564,769 - _____	1,223,530,239 - _____

35. A farm grows 3,657 bushels of wheat.
    How many bushels is that rounded off
    to the nearest thousand?

    _____

36. At one point the population of the
    United States was 209,654,768. What
    was this rounded off to the nearest
    million?

    _____

Date:_____   ENGLISH STATION   Name:_____

Plurals of nouns, 4

50

* Remember the rules about making plurals to
  write the plural of each of these nouns:

1. knife - _____   26. penny - _____

2. wheel - _____   27. fight - _____

3. dress - _____   28. lash - _____

4. tooth - _____   29. calf - _____

5. deer - _____   30. ox - _____

6. mess - _____   31. church - _____

7. navy - _____   32. belly - _____

8. life - _____   33. plant - _____

9. jelly - _____   34. city - _____

10. floor - _____   35. shelf - _____

11. fuss - _____   36. beach - _____

12. mix - _____   37. valley - _____

13. goose - _____   38. mouse - _____

14. chimney - _____   39. woman - _____

15. box - _____   40. catch - _____

16. dictionary - _____ 41. man - _____

17. monster - _____   42. dance - _____

18. tomato - _____   43. brace - _____

19. dash - _____   44. jockey - _____

20. wife - _____   45. tax - _____

21. leaf - _____   46. sheep - _____

22. monkey - _____   47. half - _____

23. child - _____   48. machine - _____

24. Negro - _____   49. wharf - _____

25. beach - _____   50. foot - _____

Date: _____   SPELLING STATION   [14]   Name: _____

* Use each word or set of words in a good sentence.

liquor - a drink with alcohol in it
_____

hockey - a game played by ice skaters with special sticks and a puck
_____

clumsy - awkward; always falling down, bumping into things, etc.
_____

orphan - a child whose mother and father are both dead
_____

protect - to keep someone or something from being hurt
_____

recover - to get better (like from a cold); also to get back something that was lost
_____

equator - the imaginary line around the middle of the world between the two poles
_____

tough - not soft or weak; can take punishment and hard times
_____

jigsaw puzzle - a puzzle with many pieces that fit together into one picture
difficult - not easy
_____

vulture - a large bird that feeds on the dead bodies of animals and people
corpse - a dead body
donkey - a tame animal of the ass family

_____

** Which word rhymes with stuff? _____

Date: _____   GENERAL STATION   [36]   Name: _____

* Put these words into groups of five that belong
  together. Then give each group a good name in
  the space at the bottom of each box.

tigers

pigs

hamsters

Minnesota

toothpaste

gerbils

Nevada

bicycle

shaving cream

rabbits

lions

train

boa constrictors

guinea pigs

cows

deodorant

automobile

Washington

sheep

elephants

turtles

rickshaw

shampoo

Wyoming

chickens

jet

soap

Illinois

lambs

leopards

Feedback— Correcting and Evaluating

Most of us have had moments when we've wondered whether the work involved in correcting papers every day is worth it, whether handing back corrected work to kids is really a learning experience for them. These doubts are especially likely to crop up when we're faced with a great stack of papers (which is keeping us from the more creative side of teaching and dominating much of our out-of-school lives), when we see kids throwing their corrected papers in the wastepaper basket without a glance at them, when kids flip through their papers looking only at their grades and comparing them to other kids' or when kids become sullen over their mistakes, taking each red mark as a comment on their character and proof that they can't do anything right. Perhaps all these reactions are really part of the same thing—kids are very sensitive about being criticized, and the correcting process may be too threatening to be very helpful to them.

One goal to work towards is for kids to have a good idea whether their answers are correct *as they do the work*. This happens when kids are motivated enough to check their work carefully as they go along, when the teacher is readily available to give help and reassurance, when kids are working on projects which they really care about and when the materials have built-in checking mechanisms or there is a readily available answer key.

When kids are involved in a five-day learning process which leads to mastery of a skill or concept or body of knowledge, the basic purpose of correcting shifts from simply giving feedback (which is still important) to that of helping the kids who are having trouble. If you have a helper in your room you can split up the people who need help, or you can group the kids with friends who will help them. You might even start a student tutoring service in the room. After a while you'll undoubtedly get a feel for the kids who need more attention in certain areas—you can anticipate their need before they call you or hand in a paper that's all wrong.

Kids are more receptive to criticism and more likely to correct answers while they are doing their work than after they have finished. Making most of the learning happen as kids do the work depends on three things: (1) the work being clear, doable and to some degree self-checking; (2) kids being willing to ask for help from you, helpers or other kids; and (3) your being highly mobile and available to give help and anticipate needs. If these three requirements are met, correcting will become less negative for the kids; if they are less threatened by red ink, they are more likely to accept the criticism contained in the corrected paper.

CHEATING—OR COOPERATION?

Another activity to encourage in your classroom is having kids who are working together compare notes when they've finished. They may discover discrepancies, and this can lead them through a real learning process, figuring out which answer is right. Of course there is a fine line between this extremely valuable learning process and simple copying, without interchange or thought—a practice which greatly dilutes any learning that is taking place. A learning station classroom makes "cheating" a lot easier because kids are sitting in groups and allowed to work together. If the room is functioning well, however, the amount of pure copying should be negligible. Here is a kid's-eye view of reasons for "cheating" and the ways a station system counteracts each one:

1. The work is boring and copying is a way of getting through it without expending useless intellectual effort. *Station materials should be relevant, exciting and fun to do, motivating kids to do the work themselves.*

2. The work is too hard and copying is a way of getting through it without admitting to the teacher or other kids that I can't do it. *Station materials should be geared to your kids, have clear instruc-*

tions and be doable by all your kids, with occasional help—so kids should be willing to try to do their own work.*

3. Since the teacher is sitting in the front of the room and can't see me, I'll copy the work and get it over with faster. *In a station class the teacher is always on the move, and is much more likely to spot kids who are copying.*

4. The teacher doesn't have time to help me—I'll copy the answers to the hard work since I can't do it by myself. *The dispersal of work through the day and the self-sufficiency of most kids in a station class should free the teacher to move around the room and give help to kids who need it.*

5. It's embarrassing to ask for help in a quiet, teacher-centered classroom; other kids might call me a dummy, so I'll copy the answers to the hard work and no one will know I'm having trouble with it. *A station classroom has a constant buzz of noise and people are usually involved in their own work. This means it's possible to have very private conferences with the teacher right in the middle of a crowded room. Kids can get plenty of help without being conspicuous and feeling embarrassed.*

6. The work is graded, grades go onto report cards and my parents are on my back about my grades—I'll copy to improve my grades and get my parents off my back, even please them. *Grades on work done during the week in a station class aren't for credit; they're given only to help kids see the kind of mistakes they're making and help them master the material by the time the test rolls around. The whole emphasis is on the student's understanding the work by the end of the week and being able to do it independently, with no help from teacher or friends.*

7. There's a lot of time pressure to get work done before the class moves on to the next subject—I'll copy so I won't be left behind. *A station class can have this problem, especially if kids know they can play games or do other, more interesting things when they finish all their work. You can work on the concomitant causes (by helping kids, getting them together with kids who will help them and improving their skills and level of self-sufficiency), but the problem of slower kids trying to do their work too fast remains. This makes it doubly important for you to know the kids who are most likely to succumb to this temptation; you can pre-empt it by helping them in their weak subjects in the early part of the day and then coming back to them with help and encouragement as the day goes on. It's also important that you check work carefully as it is handed in to make sure less motivated kids have done a thorough job. You might also want to keep certain games off-limits until*

most kids are finished with their work, and encourage kids who finish early to help their slower friends or read books, rather than going off and conspicuously playing games.

GIVING EFFECTIVE FEEDBACK

A station classroom can help combat these seven common reasons for copying, and thus increase the percentage of learning that takes place as kids do their work. But it's still important to many kids to have their work corrected and returned to them, and parents may wonder if you're doing your job when papers are not returned. Correcting papers does keep us in touch with how kids are doing, gives us a chance to appreciate the amount of work that gets done by the class during a day and a chance to get into a dialogue with our written comments. While most of our teaching should be creative (writing and finding good materials and working with kids directly during the day), correcting and giving feedback can be an important dimension.

The ideal situation is to have instant feedback—have the kids watch you correct their work the minute they finish, or watch them correct their own. Instant feedback has the advantage of reinforcing right answers and correcting wrong ones while the material is still very fresh in the kids' minds. They may be tired of the work at that point, however, and not really care about mistakes they may have made. You also may find it hard to be immediately available.

Another approach is to correct the work after class and give it back the next morning so that kids can go over it when they're rested; they can then apply the lessons to the day's work they are about to begin. But if you go over papers first thing in the morning, you'll be pitting that activity against the usual early morning socializing—looking over corrected work may come up with the short end of the stick. Better than this is to call kids up one at a time and go over their work from the previous day, pointing out mistakes and praising good ideas and good papers. This also may be hard to do first thing in the morning, with interruptions and other kids restless to begin the day's work; you might want to keep the rest of the class busy with board work or a short quiet reading time while you have the individual conferences. You can also limit individual conferences on corrected work to one day a week.

ROTATING CORRECTING METHODS

None of these methods deals with the fact that correcting seven papers from each of 25 to 30 kids is too much for most of us to do on a continual basis. If you want to limit your daily take-home work to around two hours—and want to spend most of that time creating curriculum and dreaming up new ideas and projects rather than rehashing the previous day's work—and if you want to be able to lead an active personal life, you have to find ways to cut down the time it takes to correct papers. Furthermore, kids shouldn't assume that the teacher will always do all the correcting—if they do, they won't get involved in evaluating their own work.

Four different modes of correcting can maximize the learning and minimize the intimidation factor for kids—three of them can greatly reduce your work load. The best strategy may be to rotate the four modes during the week, keeping any one from being overused and losing its effectiveness.

Mode 1 for Monday and test day   You do all the correcting and

give feedback the next morning in individual conferences. You learn who to zero in on with help that week.

Mode 2 for Tuesday A committee (with a rotating membership) of four or five kids does most of the correcting from answer sheets you have filled out. You correct the papers that don't have right or wrong answers. This can be a good learning experience for the kids who do the correcting, and if it's not overdone, most kids love to do it. You may find that they are a lot tougher on each other than you are!

Mode 3 for Wednesday You correct four or five papers orally as a class that afternoon or the next morning, reading questions and having kids call out the answers and correct their own papers. (As with any form of self-checking, look over their papers when they finish to make sure they have done a thorough job.) This has the advantage of giving kids oral reinforcement for work they've been reading silently, which is especially important in spelling and reading. There's a further advantage to having kids check their own papers—they're more likely to get a feeling of how much of the paper is *right* rather than looking straight at the questions they got wrong, as they normally do.

Mode 4 for Thursday When the kids have finished all their work, correct four or five of their own papers from answer sheets on separate desks or tables. By Thursday they should be doing well enough for this to be a confidence-building experience, but it should also show them directly and privately what kinds of mistakes they are still making. If one set of answer sheets causes too much congestion, you might write a second set, put some answers on the board or project an answer sheet, using an opaque or overhead projector. Kids, however, usually finish their work at staggered intervals, making a private correcting session a viable method.

The last three correcting modes should take a lot of work off your shoulders, and give kids more responsibility for checking their own mistakes. A rotating system can make feedback more meaningful and much more a part of the learning process.

Once liberated from endless correcting, the preparation time you spend after school can become much more productive. My approach at this point is to spend two or three hours Sunday evening collecting and writing the worksheets and assignments for the entire week. On Monday, during school hours, I run off and file the week's work, and devote the weekday nights (usually less than 90 minutes a night) to the feedback process. This work consists of looking over and correcting kids' papers; taking note of the kids who will need special help mastering concepts the next day; making lists of words to test kids on; preparing answer sheets; thinking through things to be discussed at class meetings or presented as part of lectures; clipping stories and pictures out of newspapers and magazines; preparing readings or tape recordings; and thinking about projects for individual kids.

FAILED TESTS CAN BE TAKEN AGAIN

What becomes of the grades given at the end of each week? Are they final and irrevocable, going straight into report cards, or is there a more flexible system that allows for the inevitable bad days, bad weeks or even bad months in kids' lives? A poor grade on an end-of-the-week test isn't unalterable. You can keep copies of all tests in a filing cabinet, then let the kids retake tests they failed when they think they have mastered the skill or caught up on the material. This system requires a fair amount of organizing, extra work teaching back material, supervising the individual tests and more papers to correct—but the benefits for the kids are considerable. Instead of an immutable "D" or "E" at the top of their failing test paper, kids might find a more hopeful and encouraging "Try again." If you give them the time and encouragement to do so (again, an aide or helper is invaluable), kids are likely to take advantage of this opportunity to master skills that might otherwise be buried in the rush to new work, avoiding a spiral of failure and low self-esteem.

Two weeks before the grade deadline for each report card, inform the kids of their present grades and urge them to improve their records by retaking old tests. This usually generates a flurry of activity—it may be the first time many kids have been given a second chance to get good grades.

It is important to give kids a sense of the class progressing through the curriculum, mastering skills and gradually improving —but kids also should be internally motivated, inspired by their love of learning and their satisfaction at doing well. By using the systems suggested here, kids should become less afraid of red ink and better equipped to learn from it, more able to check and evaluate their own work as they do it and less dependent on the teacher for help, feedback and encouragement. In short, kids should learn how to make the best of what future classrooms have to offer.

Group Meetings— Pulling Everything Together

In the first two years I used a learning station system, I made very few attempts to get everyone's attention at the same time; I kept a low public profile and worked out almost all class problems individually, in small groups or through worksheets. I asked kids' opinions on changing the class around in the General Station, rehashed a bad day and asked for suggestions in the Reading Station or asked kids to write about the room to get their ideas and reassurance on how things were going. This level of decentralization may have been an over-reaction to the problems of stand-up teaching, a reflection of my own lack of self-confidence and skill at running group sessions without resorting to harsh authoritarian measures.

As time went on, however, I felt the urge to share with the kids certain things which were too small or too complicated to turn into a worksheet. I also craved more of a sense of the class as a group, more verbal feedback from kids on how the class was going. It seemed that running a class without some kind of group meeting left a lot of important things to chance or kept them from happening at all. So I began to call for everyone's attention in the middle of the station time—I put on a two-minute stand-up teaching performance and fielded questions before letting kids return to their work. These little acts included stories from the news, exhortations not to embarrass me in front of visitors, interesting points raised by kids about the worksheets or just stories I was reminded of by something that was said or happened in the room. The kids usually listened very carefully because the mini-lecture was a brief and interesting break in the routine, and I usually didn't need any authoritarian methods to keep order. Had the mini-lectures been longer or less interesting, they would have lost their effectiveness. As it was, the change of pace made stand-up teaching something to be listened to and enjoyed, rather than tuned out and fought.

There was an additional advantage to these sessions—the possibility of following through with a longer discussion with a few kids who expressed an interest while everyone else went back to work. The essence of the mini-lecture is its spontaneity and flexibility—there is little pressure on you to extend an idea into a full-blown lecture or feel threatened or put down if it isn't greeted by overwhelming interest.

BRINGING HEADS TOGETHER
But mini-lectures hardly pull the class together to deal collectively with its problems and interests. It still seemed as though some kind of formal meeting and really open discussion was needed. My instinct was to keep math, English grammar and spelling out of such meetings unless they were a part of catchy and interesting ideas (i.e., games, competitions, brain teasers, etc.). I decided to limit the teaching and drilling of basic skills and subject matter to worksheets and individualized instruction. Class meetings, I thought, should focus on topics which lend themselves to discussion, to putting many heads together to generate ideas and to areas where group decisions are important to the welfare of the class.

You might want to start having class meetings right at the beginning of the year, and count on their unique participatory quality to form the contrast with teacher-dominated, hassle-filled sessions in previous years. On the other hand, you may want to have almost no all-class sessions for the first month or so of the year, letting kids settle into their groups, get to know each other and you at a personal rather than a "public" level. In this way they may develop positive feelings about the room and the way it functions while forgetting any negative associations with other classrooms or negative behaviors associated with them (tuning out or acting up). When all this has happened, the time may be ripe to start holding daily class meetings where everyone pushes desks from the small groups into a large circle, the teacher sits down (an important distinction from standing up and dominating the group) and the class discusses mutual problems, ideas, experiences, news items, plans, moral dilemmas, values and so on.

A number of educators offer help in conducting affective meetings:

1. Sidney Simon's *Values Clarification* (New York: Hart, 1972) describes a method of getting values out into the open, getting people to realize what these values mean and helping them to change or affirm them. Simon's books—*I Am Loveable and Capable* (Chicago: Argus, 1974) and *Meeting Yourself Halfway* (Chicago: Argus, 1974) —are full of specific suggestions and ideas for group meetings.

2. Lawrence Kohlberg's writings probe an intriguing hierarchy of moral stages which Kohlberg contends all people move through as they grow up. The idea behind his research is that if kids discuss their reactions to hypothetical moral dilemmas and are answered by moral reasoning one or two stages higher than their own, their own moral development will be accelerated. You can get *Hypothetical Moral Dilemmas* ($5.00) and *A Handbook for Assessing Moral Reasoning* ($2.00) by writing Moral Education Research Foundation, Harvard School of Education, Larsen Hall, Cambridge, Mass. 02138. (All orders should be prepaid.) Kohlberg's work also is explored in "First Things: Values," a set of filmstrips prepared by Kohlberg in consultation with Robert L. Selman (Pleasantville, N.Y.: Guidance Associates, 1972).

3. William Glasser describes still another technique in his book, *Schools Without Failure* (New York: Harper & Row, 1969). His approach offers a method of getting feelings to the surface and leading kids to share and deal with them honestly, without fear of ridicule.

4. Dr. Thomas Gordon's class rule-setting meeting ideas (*Teacher Effectiveness Training*, [New York: Wyden, 1974]) provide excellent ideas and guidelines for getting kids to formulate their own rules; they help kids work towards a classroom where rules are enforced without the teacher exerting authority. Gordon's book is also full of ideas on handling problem situations, both in individual conferences and in group meetings.

Besides these books and ideas you can also use the old stand-bys brainstorming, role playing, charades, spelling bees and guessing games to pull kids together, give them a sense of group and a chance to express themselves to the whole class.

As Thomas Gordon points out, effective class meetings which discuss problems can provide the best instruction in democratic principles (as opposed to dry lectures and civics textbooks). Waiting your turn in a group situation, listening to the ideas and opinions of others and forming a group consensus are all lessons that are best learned through participation. If a decentralized classroom is an ideal setting for shy kids to come out of their shells and begin to express themselves, a well-run class meeting is an ideal setting for more articulate kids to make their opinions felt, and a proving ground for the new-found self-confidence of others. If the station classroom really helps kids get along, form close bonds and learn to deal with conflict peacefully, the class meeting is a time for them to see that new-found cooperation working out in the open—by seeing it they can internalize it, and make it a part of their lives.

STAYING CALM—AND USING ALL-CLASS INSTRUCTION SPARINGLY

The teacher's role in the class meeting is that of leader, not pedant or authority figure—by leading you can help kids express themselves; mirror and decode emotions so their real content can be discussed; restate anger and conflict in a way that it can be dealt with; come up with good ideas and suggestions and provide the energy to keep a meeting on the tracks (or the wisdom to stop it if it's irrevocably off the tracks). One measure of how effective your role in a class meeting has been might be to ask yourself afterwards how many times you had to use your power as a teacher, how often you had to pull rank or threaten punishment or promise rewards, to keep the meeting going. The more you did, the less valuable the meeting probably was in terms of academic and human relations and civics objectives.

Though academic subjects don't belong in the class meeting, they may benefit from all-class instruction. I've often called a class together to go over a difficult concept, read over spelling words, read a story aloud that the kids had already read silently or correct papers as a group with kids calling out the answers. Sessions like these can be effective if they are brisk and fast-moving, and they may provide important oral reinforcement for kids who have been doing most of their work silently. But I try to minimize group sessions and find other ways of teaching the actual subject matter. I ask myself whether an all-class session is the most effective way to accomplish an academic or human relations goal I have in mind, or whether there's a better, more efficient way of doing the same thing. For instance, am I talking to the whole class just to kill time, or because I'm worried the kids will be too noisy if I don't control them? (Perhaps I should plan more activities, provide more things for the kids to do in their spare time and hold class meetings on keeping noise within acceptable limits.) Am I going over papers with the group because I don't want to correct them myself? Do the kids really learn anything from such a group correcting? (Perhaps I should let the kids correct their own papers from an answer sheet at the front of the room or from an overhead transparency projected on a screen, have a few kids correct the papers for me or call kids up one at a time to go over their work.) Is anything being gained by reading this story to the whole class? Will it stir interest and start a discussion, or is it merely a repeat performance of kids' own silent reading, basically a prima donna performance that is resented by many kids, tuned out by others? (If so, then I should encourage kids to read stories out loud to each other, or listen to kids read in small groups.) Is going over this new concept on the board really teaching it to the kids who will have trouble with it, or will I end up still having to go around the room explaining it to each of them individually? (If so, I should find good self-instructing materials or write my own step-by-step worksheets.)

Sometimes it seems that negative sessions and confrontations between teachers and kids are inevitable, and the only alternative to chaos or embarrassment or an unhealthy bottling up of strong feelings or evil moods. They are especially likely to happen when we haven't planned properly, when there is time pressure that precludes a civilized discussion or when outside factors (schedule changes, unexpected visitors, etc.) disrupt routines or make us self-conscious about what is happening in the room. But we should always work towards eliminating these negative scenes and make our contacts with the whole class reflect these central purposes:

1. getting kids together and giving them a sense of being a class
2. getting kids to express themselves more freely and effectively
3. leading kids to listen to the ideas and opinions of others (including yours)
4. dealing with problems collectively and democratically, and giving kids a feeling that they *can* solve problems themselves without an authority figure stepping in
5. giving the teacher a chance to tell kids interesting stories and experiences and ideas
6. giving the teacher a chance to escape being a shouter and an authority figure, and become an effective role model of a leader, source of good ideas and patient listener
7. giving *all* the kids a chance to participate and learn something —not just the quicker students

Free Time

There's a feeling among some parents and administrators that kids should be working every minute of the school day—if they're not, the teacher isn't doing the job properly. Such an attitude combines a desire to "get your money's worth" out of school, a fear of what kids will do with free time ("The idle mind is the devil's playground") and the idea that the curriculum is infinite. But trying to keep kids busy all day doesn't encourage them to work very hard, doesn't teach them much about using and planning free time and doesn't give them much time to interact with each other.

The conventional work-saturated school day encourages a foot-dragging, "slow-the-teacher-down" ethos among kids; there is little incentive to get work done and nothing to be gained by finishing more quickly but more work (a prospect which only a small minority of self-motivated kids finds inspiring). I'm convinced that it's possible for kids to do a lot of work in a small amount of time—and attack the work with gusto, getting more out of it—by keeping the amount of work finite and using free time as an incentive. Most people who are horrified by free time in the classroom just don't realize how many hours there are in a school day, or how fast kids can work when they are properly motivated. Given the right motivation, the question is not whether kids will get through the required curriculum, but whether the teacher can provide enough for them to do within and beyond the curriculum. (For more on covering requirements, see Chapter 5.)

When given a finite amount of work and a large block of time in which to do it, most people (adults as well as kids) react in one of two ways: they put the work off until the last minute and enjoy the guilty pleasures of free time before buckling down; or they do the work quickly, getting it out of the way and enabling themselves to enjoy the free time without work hanging over them. With some prodding (and a judicious limiting of access to some free time activities in the early part of the day) you can get most kids into the second pattern; they'll soon discover the satisfaction of getting out from under their work and the rewards of having time to do other things.

After a few weeks of a station program, kids usually get into the routine of working very hard in the morning to earn free time later in the day. As time passes, more and more kids learn how to work on their own, getting help when they need it from you and from their friends, and they finish their work earlier and earlier in the day. The incentive of free time and a finite amount of work acts to compress into much less time what would normally be more than a full day's work. If things are going well, kids will throw themselves into the work and really enjoy the process of getting it done.

BUT WHAT IF THEY FINISH TOO EARLY?

There's a temptation to heap more work on those kids who finish early, keeping them out of your hair and alleviating the guilt you may feel that they are wasting time. But to do this would undermine the whole incentive system. By taking away the prospect of free time, you are likely to produce a foot-dragging, time-killing and even disruptive pattern of behavior in these kids, and take a lot of the fun out of doing the day's work. Putting more work on an early finisher also has the disadvantage of seeming unfair—"How come I have to do more work when the rest of the kids just have to do seven assignments?" or "If I finish my work faster, I deserve some free time!" It's hard to answer these arguments; extra work is going to seem like a punishment or just busy work unless the kids are really eager to do it on their own.

There are two additional problems with piling more work on those who finish early: the logistics of planning and correcting the extra work so it's meaningful and not just busy work, and the difficulty of deciding at what point kids who are finishing their work are not assigned further work (or does everyone have to keep working

until the last student has finished the stations?). Clearly it's easier and more effective to leave the free time open for voluntary activities; you can stock the room with a number of games and project ideas which kids can do without a lot of direction from the teacher and without disturbing the kids who are still working.

Using free time as an incentive has the potential of resulting in rushed, sloppy work from the kids. This makes it vital that you check over everyone's work as it is finished, and always send back work that isn't up to your standards. Checking work seems easiest if the papers are stapled in a prearranged, fixed order (math, English, social studies, spelling, etc.) and if I look at certain selected questions as I flip through, as well as check for neatness and completeness. Catching errors and omissions at this stage and having kids correct them immediately is much more effective than correcting the papers later and handing them back the next day. (For more on feedback, see Chapter 6.) Since kids usually finish their work in a staggered succession through the middle section of the day, you should have time to give most of them some quick, individual feedback on the day's work at the moment they finish.

SOME WILL HAVE MORE FREE TIME THAN OTHERS
In a conventional one-period, one-subject system, a dual problem often arises—fast kids finish early and get bored, while slow kids feel pressured to hurry through the work, not doing their best. The

teacher is usually caught in the middle, trying to appease the kids who have finished and prod the kids who haven't. In a station system, kids attack their work all at once. Fast kids can "save up" all the time they gain on each subject and "spend" it all at once in a large block of free time when they have finished all the stations (rather than in small, confining five- or ten-minute pieces at the end of each lesson). Slow kids, on the other hand, can get more concentrated help with subjects they have trouble with, and won't feel rushed or that they're holding up the class. Free time acts as a cushion for the different lengths of time it takes kids to do their work.

It's one of the built-in inequalities of a system like this that some kids will have much more free time than others. You have to decide whether this disadvantage outweighs all the advantages or whether there are any alternatives that work better. Giving less work to the slower kids so they can finish more nearly at the same time as the others can undermine the incentive system and indirectly encourage those kids who aren't highly motivated to work more slowly— that way they will have their work cut back too. After a while it may be difficult for you to identify the kids who really need to be given a break on their work. Giving less work to the slow kids also runs the risk of publicly identifying a "dumb" group in the class, damaging egos which cannot afford it. You may also unwittingly convey the message that you don't want to help certain kids or want them to improve.

ATTENTION AND ENCOURAGEMENT WILL HELP
THE SLOWER WORKER

To help slower kids get more easily through the day, give them plenty of attention and help in the early part of the day with the papers they find hardest; with the worst behind them, they can face the easier work later on. You can keep a defeatist attitude from developing with lots of encouragement and confidence-building pep talks. You can also encourage slower kids to sit with friends who work quickly, and urge the faster students to help their slower-working friends.

Keeping game playing quiet and, if possible, out of sight, may be another way to ease the frustrations of the slower workers—late finishers won't be constantly reminded that others are having fun while they toil away. Important, too, is making sure that everyone has at least some free time; try to engineer the day so that even the slowest kids can finish and have time to relax and enjoy the fruits of their labor.

Free time inequalities can't be avoided—but you can mitigate the resulting problems by making use of all the resources and advantages the system has to offer. Don't try to eliminate all differences between kids—do try to work with them on their specific problems and frustrations. Experiment until you find a way to bring the inequalities of working time within an acceptable range. Then free time can be the best kind of motivation for improving classroom skills. (For more on individualization, see Chapter 10.)

A VARIETY OF FREE TIME ACTIVITIES

The best way to minimize problems in the after-stations part of the day is to stock your classroom with lots of activities and put a list of suggestions on the wall to guide and stimulate kids in using them. Here is a list of the kinds of things that might fill free time with interesting and mildly educational activity (some kids may actually learn more in their free time than they did from the "official" work!):

1. books of all kinds and all reading levels—novels, comics, mysteries, sports, picture books, etc.

2. magazines of all kinds—*Mad, The Electric Company Magazine, Ebony, Sports Illustrated, Cricket, Car and Driver, Boys' Life, Popular Mechanics, Ebony Jr!, People, Kids, Cracked, National Geographic, Time, Newsweek,* etc.

3. newspapers—at least two dailies for that day

4. mazes (copied or with an acetate overlay and grease pencils to re-use the original)

5. art projects and a well-stocked art corner

6. reading plays in small groups, with copies of good plays available

7. listening to stories or plays recorded on a cassette tape recorder (using headsets) and reading along with the original text

8. listening to songs and reading along with the lyrics

9. working out math problems on a calculator

10. correcting papers for the teacher

11. retaking tests that were failed the first time

12. writing stories or writing thoughts in a diary or journal

13. editing a class magazine

14. holding small-group discussions on moral dilemmas, news stories, class problems, etc.

15. building models and patterns with cubes or other material

16. typing

17. playing popular board games

18. a "Question of the Day" contest with one question each day (i.e., Why is a plane's wing shaped the way it is or Why is the ocean blue?) that requires research; kids accumulate points toward a

monthly prize

19. helping other kids with their work or tutoring them on skills they don't understand

20. any other reasonable building, sewing, knitting, weaving, acting, carving, pasting, shaping or calculating project you or your kids have the resources and time for

All these activities can be defended as an extension of the "academic" curriculum if parents or administrators question their use. You also have the defense that the incentive of free time has made it possible to compress a full day's work into less time, allowing both work and play, and maximizing the chances of kids learning one way or the other.

Of course, the free time activities can also be seen as just plain fun, without worrying about what kids are learning. Their most important benefit, however, may be strengthened human relations —they give kids time to practice getting along together without direct supervision, time to play, decide, debate, argue, compete, talk, joke, work and think together. Given a controlled environment and plenty of cooperative and interesting things to do, free time activity can be the most effective kind of human relations training you can offer. (This may be especially important in newly integrated situations. Kids may resent and resist being pushed together, discussing race relations in the abstract, doing gimmicky encounter exercises or being lectured on racial and ethnic harmony. They may, however, get along famously as soon as they have some open time and some fun things to do together.)

A QUIET READING TIME

But what happens when all the great games and activities go stale from overuse, and the free time period becomes noisy and negative? One idea is to schedule a quiet reading time at the end of each day, right at the time when people begin to lose their sense of humor and the atmosphere of harmony and goodwill begins to fray at the edges. About an hour before the end of the school day, you might start the process of cleaning up the room and tell the kids they have ten minutes to find a book they want to read. You might tell them how important reading is, and that it's worthy of some special time. Then, with about 45 minutes of school left, ask that there be absolutely no talking or noise or moving around the room. After 30 or 35 minutes of quiet reading, kids can put their books back and get ready to go home.

Getting a quiet reading time going usually requires a certain amount of sternness from the teacher, especially if it immediately follows a free-wheeling game and project time. But once the principle of absolute quiet has been established, there's usually a genuine sense of relief and relaxation. The result should be that you end the day on a more positive note, and that your kids do a lot more reading than they would in an extended free time.

It's tempting for us to use this quiet reading time to get a head start on the day's correcting. There's something wrong, however, with telling kids that reading is important enough for a whole reading period and then proceeding to do something else ourselves. I think it is crucial that the teacher act as a model for kids and spend the reading time doing the same thing as everyone else—getting totally immersed in a good book. Some schools have taken this a step further and set up daily 45-minute blocks of time when everyone in the whole school, including custodians, secretaries and administrators, sits down and reads a book.

Of course the main purpose of a quiet reading time is not to shut kids up at a difficult point in the day or limit the use of games to keep them from going stale—it's to get kids hooked on books. Ideally, with lots of good books and magazines displayed around a classroom and plenty of free time, kids would read without having a special time set aside for it. But there are three reasons why this usually doesn't happen. First, there is too much noise and activity around the room for most kids to settle down and read, no matter how much they may want to and how interesting the reading matter might be; most kids need a really quiet, placid atmosphere to get involved in leisure reading. Second, there are too many competing activities—games and projects tend to outbid reading because their rewards are more immediate and social, while reading's are personal and cerebral. And third, it's not "cool" to many kids to read by themselves when their friends are doing other more active things around the room. Many kids need the support of their peers (sometimes only achieved by the compulsion of the teacher) to settle down and get involved in a book—but under that condition their involvement may become complete. In other words, kids may actually be grateful to you for setting up the quiet reading time.

Should you require weekly book reports to make sure kids are really reading their books? Book reports are one way of checking up, but the ideal is to have a half-hour or so of open time for kids to read purely for enjoyment, without any academic pressures to race through the book and write something about it. A real leisure reading time seems like the best way to begin the process of getting kids hooked on reading for its own sake.

At first glance, the quiet reading time seems authoritarian (no noise, reading only), but for the reasons just cited it may be the best way to get kids into books. As time goes on, it should become less and less difficult to get the quiet reading time started, and kids should build up more and more desire to read books without such a structure. There may come a time when the structure can just wither away and kids will happily read despite the social and environment pressures.

How to Work With Others

A TWO-ROOM TEAM ARRANGEMENT

There are a number of advantages in getting together with another like-minded teacher and running two station classrooms in tandem, sharing resources and creative effort. Two teachers can share the job of writing and collecting materials, getting movies and filmstrips, dreaming up projects, arranging field trips, bringing in visitors, organizing plays, setting up contests and debates, decorating, buying paperbacks and magazines, finding good stories to read out loud and all the other things that may seem overwhelming to one teacher all alone. Each teacher can also provide invaluable moral support when the other is at a low ebb, a sense of perspective (and hopefully humor) on problems and a person to talk with about common problems—in short, a team teacher can help alleviate the feeling of isolation that often bedevils the self-contained classroom teacher.

The ideal team-teaching arrangement is two rooms with an adjoining door—this allows a flow of students and adults from one room to the other, but a door to close for class meetings and a sense of privacy. Two adjoining classrooms can also provide two different atmospheres, and some kids may appreciate being able to move from one to another. Restless kids will be able to move into another room rather than disrupt your room or venture into the school corridors. Kids can be temporarily transferred to the other room if there's an irreconcilable personality clash or a particularly noisy friendship that needs cooling off. If kids in both rooms know the limits and resources and people on both sides of the door, an informal exchange program can spring up and operate throughout the year, expanding the options for kids and easing the pressure on both teachers to be all things to all people.

If your routines are well enough established and you have an aide or a student teacher, it also may be possible for you to take small groups of kids on field trips while your colleague keeps an eye on both rooms (the next time you switch roles). This not only increases the value of field trips because of the small size of the group, but it also gives the remaining kids valuable practice in doing without the direct supervision of their own teacher—who is, after all, someone they must learn to live without.

There are countless ways of arranging the interaction between two classrooms. At the most separate level, the door between them could remain closed and the cooperation consist only of a sharing of ideas and materials between the two teachers (in this case the two rooms could be down the hall from one another or even in separate buildings). Or you might want to keep the door closed for the morning, each class having its own private class meeting and learning station time, and then open it to a free flow between the two rooms during the free time, when the most interaction is possible. If all the books are in one room and all the games in the other, the flow between them is maximized and kids can choose their friends and activities from a larger selection.

Another possibility is to hold a joint class meeting every morning and then let the station time straddle both rooms, with kids being given the choice of teacher and atmosphere (or the teachers circulating between the two rooms, helping their homeroom students). In this case, kids might not consider themselves as belonging to one room or the other, but as members of a two-room community. The rooms might come to serve quite different functions—one a quiet work, reading and plant-growing room, the other a more active game-playing, typing, experimenting, building and animal-cage room. It's likely, however, that many kids may want more security and more of a sense of place than this kind of arrangement provides —their own table in their own room with one group of friends and their own teacher.

A two-room team arrangement might be the beginning of bigger things; larger teams or whole corridors could be organized and coordinated, classroom walls ignored and ideas and energies pooled on a larger scale. The keys to success are finding compatible people and an environment which provides the right mixture of adventure and security, novelty and familiarity and freedom and structure, for adults and students alike.

FIELD TRIPS

Even in the midst of a scintillating year in the classroom, with hundreds of successful learning experiences, one good field trip may stand out as the most powerful memory in a kid's mind. The impact of the real world, experienced firsthand, is unmatched by any book, movie or slide show—we should all be field trip enthusiasts, getting our students to factories, museums, forests, aquariums, skyscrapers, business offices, nature trails and zoos on every possible occasion.

I've never thought that the most important part of a field trip was whether it fitted into a particular unit the class was doing or whether the kids did a detailed rehash of its meaning when they came back (although all of that is good and enhances a field trip's value). The most important thing, I think, is being able to get up close to milking machines, automatic bread wrappers and printing presses—and being able to ask plenty of questions to a teacher who knows what is going on (e.g., has taken the tour before), and doesn't have to worry about shepherding 30 kids. This means small groups, five or six at the most, which in turn means that trips have to be either after school, on Saturdays or during school while a team colleague, aide or sympathetic administrator holds down the fort. (It's important to convince the kids who are left behind that there will be more trips and that everyone will get a turn. Select kids for each trip not on the basis of their behavior—when a teacher threatens to keep kids from going on a field trip because of bad behavior, their obligatory response is "Well, we didn't want to go on your cheap field trip anyway!"—but on the basis of their interests.)

While public transportation is the most ecological way to travel on a field trip, it's seldom the fastest or the most convenient. The ideal arrangement is to use a school bus or your own car, after getting written permission from parents and checking that insurance policies cover kids in transit. Unfortunately, most insurance policies on private cars don't cover all risks, and you run the risk of being involved in an accident and having the parent of an injured child sue you, should you go without proper coverage. Many teachers won't take trips in their own cars because of this risk, and there's a clear need for an insurance policy that will cover "teacher as driver" field trips.

AIDES, STUDENT TEACHERS, PARENTS AND OTHER HELPERS

When kids are involved in their small-group work, asking questions as they encounter problems, it sometimes seems as though ten helpers wouldn't be enough to meet the demand for attention. An aide, a parent volunteer, student teacher or student from a higher grade can provide another person to answer questions, give opinions to and offer a different shoulder to cry on. (A helper may also make it easier to take small groups on field trips during school hours, as previously described.) Two adults in a classroom may be able to divide between them the kids who need the most help, or agree that one will be mobile and answer the many little questions around the room while the other sits down and works with kids who need more sustained attention.

With a large demand for help from a sizable group of kids and the increased paper work generated by the learning stations, it would seem evident that the more helpers there were, the better the classroom would run. But there are some limitations to the number of helpers you seek out that are worth thinking about. First, you must be able to get along with your helpers, working smoothly and harmoniously with them—this will restrain kids from the temptation to try to drive a wedge between you or exploit differences of approach. This means that helpers have to fully understand the system and materials you are using and agree with your classroom methods. They also have to have the time to meet with you outside the hurly-burly of the classroom to coordinate strategy and discuss differences.

A second cautionary note is that kids may get spoiled if they can get immediate help just by snapping their fingers—they may not feel the need to read directions and figure things out for themselves. But being spoiled is less a factor of the number of helpers in the room than of the kind of help they're willing to give. You and your helpers have to agree not to answer questions that kids should be able to figure out for themselves; prod kids to read directions out loud and come to answers themselves, with a minimum of direct help from the adult. Give hints and narrow choices, and try to tread the narrow pathway between giving away too much and making things too frustrating.

If you're careful about these possibilities, having a helper in the room can open up new vistas and greatly increase your effectiveness.

By taking some of the pressure off the teacher to do everything and be everywhere, the presence of a helper may very well be synergistic—two people together may accomplish more than they could separately.

ADMINISTRATORS, SUPERVISORS, COLLEAGUES, VISITORS AND UPTIGHT PARENTS

If you're the first to attempt an open classroom in your school or if open education has a bad reputation in your community, you may get much more critical scrutiny than if your students were sitting in zombie-like silence all day and learning absolutely nothing. It's important to be prepared for any kind of criticism so you won't be put on the defensive or nonplused by it, or constantly worried about people popping into your room "at the wrong moment." I've always worked on the assumption that the most hostile visitor will appear at the worst possible moment, and have prepared myself to justify everything that is going on even then.

The most common demands of critics are for tight discipline, no encroachment by noise or disruption on other classrooms, no more than the usual demands on school administrators and counselors and concrete evidence that the curriculum is being covered and learning is taking place. If a noisy room may threaten your freedom of action, it's vital that your kids know the full story and understand your position. If they don't, you may feel bitterly resentful towards your students when they are noisy and act up. Confront your kids in a class meeting with the realities: "I'd like to have a happy class-

room where people have certain freedoms and in which I don't have to be mean and shout all the time to make you behave and learn. If it's noisy, I'm going to get in trouble with the principal and my supervisor and they're sure to make me go back to teaching the old way, which means a loss of freedom for you. Now what can we do to prevent this from happening?" If the meeting is handled well, kids should have no trouble understanding the situation and determine to keep their classroom in business. Then you are in a much better position to quietly remind them of the group consensus when things start to go wrong.

You might also want to discuss with your kids the fact that administrators and other teachers draw a lot of conclusions from the behavior of a class when the teacher is absent. You should talk about how they can handle themselves when you are out sick or away from the class. It might be somewhat irksome if your kids behaved *better* when you were gone than when you were there, but that would certainly boost your credibility among administrators and other teachers!

If a learning station system is running well, it should be obvious to visitors that learning is going on, that kids are getting along with each other and that they are enjoying their classroom rather than fighting the teacher. Most observers should be able to see that the involvement of kids within their groups far outweighs the noise and movement around the room, that the kids are working well within the invisible limits and that the room is on a kind of automatic pilot as the teacher talks to the visitor. Some visitors may actually be grateful that all eyes don't turn on them when they walk in—it can be quite intimidating for even the most self-confident adult to be suddenly fixed by 30 sets of appraising eyes when entering a teacher-centered classroom.

For those visitors who remain skeptical, it's usually effective to stress three important parts of the station system: all kids must finish all the work by the end of the day; tests for credit are given at the end of each week; and every iota of the curriculum as well as many additional topics and activities are being covered. You might want to have a student pick up a set of the day's assignments to give the visitor an idea of the quantity and rigor of a day's work.

As for your demands on the disciplinary and counseling services of the school, a station system should make people wonder why there is so little trouble in your room. If your kids are talking their problems out and forming close friendships, if you are an active, mobile and effective personality around the room and if your class meetings are going well, your room should be more or less self-sufficient, only needing outside help in real emergencies. You'll attract attention mainly for positive accomplishments and projects. More than anything else, the relative lack of conflict may open people's minds to the learning station system.

It's more than likely that the presence of a more open classroom may be hard for some of your colleagues to take, especially if their kids are asking them why their classes can't be the same way. It's possible that the presence of your class may force some teachers to re-examine their methods; it may also drive them deeper into authoritarian ways, feeling unable or unwilling to change or see themselves handling the noise, activity and personal demands of teaching a more open classroom.

I can think of three possible approaches in a situation like this. The first involves keeping to yourself, trying to make your classroom work well without being concerned about its impact on the rest of the school. This might involve forming alliances with like-minded teachers and getting into two- or three-room team arrangements. The second method involves charm and persuasion, forming good personal relationships with teachers of different philosophies, sharing materials and ideas with them and trying to sway them by your example. The third approach involves confrontation—challenging other teachers to have their classes take the same before-and-after achievement tests as yours and see how the different methods compare. It's up to you to decide whether to be a crusader or not—but if people are going to change at all, it will most likely happen by seeing a working model operating calmly and cheerfully close by, not by having it crammed down their throats. The third approach, however, might be an introduction to some kind of accountability in your school, greatly improving the quality of education for many more kids than you can teach in your own classroom.

Whenever you must justify new methods to hostile critics who have power over your freedom of action, the basic fact to realize is that you have to meet their minimum standards before moving on to pursue your own high ideals. Hopefully, learning stations will provide the necessary order, hard work and coverage of skills and curriculum with plenty of time to spare for your own projects and affective goals. The system may have one more important advantage—it's easy to explain to people, and sounds logical and fair.

Of course, eager, happy kids are the best advertisement for any system of teaching, and parents will be the first to notice if their kids are enjoying school and looking forward to leaving the house every school day. If your classroom is running well, your students will be walking protagonists of the merits of your teaching, and that, more than anything you can do, will convince the skeptics.

The Individual Needs of Kids

A station system like the one described here is not individualized in the usual sense of the word. Every child does the same seven learning assignments, and there are no explicit provisions for the individual differences that exist in every classroom. At first glance, a station classroom seems open to the criticism that it isn't meeting different kids' needs, that it should be replaced with a system that has several different levels of work in every subject and allows kids to proceed at their own level and pace. According to this school of thought, a single-level curriculum forces kids into a narrow mold and is at best the product of necessity for a teacher who doesn't have the resources to provide a truly individualized curriculum.

A station system, however, is not an old-fashioned series of blackboard lessons that leaves the quick kids yawning, the slower kids gnashing their teeth with frustration and everyone offended by having to do the same work at the same time. A station class prevents these problems and meets individual needs—but it does so as kids do their work and after they've finished, rather than by gearing the materials to different levels.

The principal mechanism of individualization in the station class is the different amounts of help you give, according to individual needs. Kids who find the work difficult or can't work effectively on their own receive a good deal of your help and encouragement, while kids who can do the work alone do so, and earn time for enrichment projects. If you are mobile and effective in giving hints and prodding, and if you train kids to help each other without copying, most individual needs will be met.

There are usually some kids who don't speak up and ask for help even though they need it, and others who will copy their friends' papers rather than go through a learning process; after a few test failures (or sooner) you should be able to find out who these people are, and begin to zero in on them in the subsequent weeks. For those who finish their work before the others there are numerous enrichment activities with which you have stocked the room. If some kids find the work too easy, they can be encouraged to extend or think up new projects for the material they're working with or tutor slower kids—a process which may be the most valuable learning experience you can provide.

WORKSHEETS AND FEEDBACK ARE A PART OF INDIVIDUALIZATION

A single-level curriculum can be individualized in another sense: many worksheets can be used at more than one level, and kids of different abilities can use the same sheet in different ways. For instance, a spelling paper which asks kids to use words in sentences can be used to write simple sentences, elaborate sentences or write whole stories using all the words together—depending on the ability of the student doing the paper. A reading paper's questions can be answered in the exact words of the original text, in the kids' own words after checking back to the story or in lengthy, personal answers without looking back to the story at all. And of course any kind of writing or open-ended project automatically caters to the different needs of kids if you constantly urge them to do the best they can.

Over a period of weeks, as you spend large amounts of time with kids who have learning problems, they should improve in terms of self-confidence, independence and thoroughness. This in turn may give you the time to embark on projects that were out of the question before, opening up new avenues of independent learning for everyone in the room. As described in Chapter 6, feedback is another form of individualization. It, too, can be an important part of meeting individual needs and getting the very most out of a single-level curriculum.

In sum, a station class can be effectively individualized if these conditions are met:

1. The teacher moves around the room and delivers widely differing amounts of help, making it possible for everyone to be able to do the work.

2. Kids help each other constructively.

3. There are plenty of activities, projects and things to read when the kids finish their work.

4. Kids are motivated by the content of the material, the leadership of the teacher and the incentive of free time; they are encouraged to do their best, thereby getting the most out of the materials.

5. Some of the materials are flexible so that different kids can get different levels of instruction from them.

6. The correcting process gives kids individual feedback on their own mistakes and a chance to think about and learn from them.

ON THE WAY TO A TRULY OPEN CLASSROOM

In Chapter 1 I spoke of the learning station system as a way station to a more open, individualized classroom. I also mentioned several conditions that prevent good open classrooms from being set up by any but the most exceptional teachers. Clearly a classroom in which kids aren't limited to a single set of assignments has greater possibilities for individual accomplishment and much more flexibility, and that's the direction in which most of us probably want to move. But it's important to be aware of the requirements that have to be met before most of us can make our classrooms truly open; with this awareness we can concentrate on a long-term program of preparing the ground:

1. We have to be superbly equipped with materials at all levels which kids can do without constant supervision. This means years of writing our own units and locating the really good commercially published materials.

2. Our students have to be independent and eager to learn, able to do their best without a stiff work requirement like the one in a station system. Teachers at every grade level must build kids' motivation and independence, helping them along the way.

3. We must be able to meet the minimum standards of our school, which means being highly organized and having the resources to give an extra push to kids who fall behind.

4. We need efficient ways to correct masses of assignments, which means having answer keys prepared and kids able and motivated to correct a lot of their own work. This again takes cooperation and energy at every grade level.

5. We have to be trained and prepared to keep track of all the different activities going on around the room. We also must be

equipped to hold individual conferences with kids to plan their programs, which means workshops, the services of one or more helpers and kids who are used to handling themselves in an unstructured classroom.

6. We need kids who can work with each other without giving answers away, and are willing to help all their classmates, not just their friends. Once again, this takes practice at every grade level.

7. We need kids who won't feel that they are being put down if they are given easier work or elevated if they are given more difficult work. This takes years in which teachers have de-emphasized competition and grades and emphasized respect and concern for each other's personalities, needs and interests.

8. We need kids who are motivated to go beyond the curriculum and pursue their interests without the direct supervision of a teacher or the structure of learning materials. Again this means years of good teachers who have aroused and assisted in developing kids' interests.

9. We need the skills to run really effective class meetings. This means years of experience running meetings and working with kids who have been participating in such meetings themselves.

All this implies active cooperation with teachers in the grades below and above our own—meetings to agree on basic academic and human relations objectives for each grade level; committees to write and buy the very best individualized materials; cooperation with parents and community agencies; and effective in-service and teacher training programs. As these conditions are slowly fulfilled in our classrooms, it may become possible to remove the elements of compulsion in a learning station system (the work requirement, the limitation to one set of materials, the quiet reading time, the group testing periods) and open our classes to more truly open education. In a few years we might be running classes in which kids pinpoint their own weaknesses, get the resources and materials and help needed to overcome them, plan their own programs, choose their own reading, conduct their own meetings, negotiate their conflicts intelligently and work together in peace. Our challenge is to find the best ways to move our kids and our classrooms towards these goals—starting now.